MERDEKA AND MUCH MORE

MERDEKA AND MUCH MORE

The Reminiscences of a
Raffles Professor
1953–67

K.G. Tregonning

MEMOIR

NUS PRESS
SINGAPORE

© 2010 NUS Press
National University of Singapore
AS3-01-02, 3 Arts Link
Singapore 117569

Fax: (65) 6774-0652
E-mail: nusbooks@nus.edu.sg
Website: http://www.nus.edu.sg/nuspress

ISBN 978-9971-69-422-7 (Paper)

National Library Board Singapore Cataloguing in Publication Data

Tregonning, K.G.
    Merdeka and much more: the reminiscences of a Raffles Professor, 1953–67 /
K.G. Tregonning. – Singapore: NUS Press, c2010.
    p. cm.
    Includes index.
    ISBN-13: 978-9971-69-422-7 (pbk.)

    1. Tregonning, K.G. 2. Singapore – History – 20th century. 3. Singapore –
Politics and government – 20th century. 4. College teachers – Singapore –
Anecdotes. 5. Historians – Singapore – Anecdotes. I. Title.

DS610.63
959.5705092 — dc22   OCN433894498

Typeset by: Scientifik Graphics
Printed by: Mainland Press Pte Ltd

To Judy

There is no mention of you anywhere in this book, but you are on every page.

Contents

List of Illustrations

Home Port

Singapore, early morning, July 22, 1953. Engines stopped, we wallow on a sluggish sea. A signal "Pilot Wanted" flies from our masthead. Tropical warmth with the dawn, banks of clouds to the east. Singapore stretches some miles along her waterfront, waiting for us. A white-painted Messageries Maritime troop ship crosses behind us as she heads for the South China Sea; her cargo of conscripted soldiers to be unloaded in Saigon in French Indo-China. Ahead, already entering Keppel Harbour is a new post war P&O passenger liner returning to England from Hong Kong, another outpost of Empire. A score of ships are at anchor in the Roads, a stream of Tongkangs entering or leaving the river to service them. A Malayan Airways twin engine DC3 — the peace time adaption of the Douglas Dakota, so well known to me — descends over us, her flight from Penang and Kuala Lumpur now ending, to land at the city's pre-war Kallang airport, just ahead of us. A busy scene.

A two-masted Bugis or Macassarese schooner drifts round St. Johns Island, one of a fleet that has traded annually with the port since it was established in 1819. A Hokkien-manned junk, overloaded with mangrove cut up a Johor river creeps down from Changi point. Its smuggled opium passed before the dawn to a Hakka fisherman crouched at the end of his lighted kelong, the lines of stakes running out to sea with his hut at the end just visible from the deck of our ship.

Leaning on the rail I reflect on Singapore's famous free port status established by Stamford Raffles. Where, I wondered, did he get the idea? I had heard, rather faintly, of a Dutch Island in the West Indies that had made a fortune in the 1770s by opening its port to ships of any nation free of any import or export charges.

The American Revolutionaries in particular obtained large quantities of much needed powder and shot from it. St. Eustatius — that was its name. Did Raffles hear of it from the Dutch while he was in Java? I never did discover what had inspired him to go against world common practice (nor has anyone else, as far as I know); but looking now at the bustling waterfront and a crowded city behind it I can see the result.

A pilot launch nudges alongside. We — a small coastal steamer of the Blue Funnel line on her regular run back from Fremantle in Western Australia — edge into our accustomed home port berth near the entrance to the three miles of wharves, passing close to the line of wrecks, salvaged after the recent war to form a breakwater to the harbour.

A small kampong of *orang laut*, Singapore's original inhabitants, juts into the water off Pulau Brani, on our port side. One of its *koleh* sails near as we make fast. Tamil labourers swarm on board, hatch covers are removed, our cargo of sheep is hurried ashore. Another Singapore day has begun, another expatriate has arrived; but this one in all humility anxious to learn, and to understand and help the Asian youths entrusted to his care, an innocent Australian, half in love already with his new home.

After three years of post-graduate study on Southeast Asia at Oxford and in London, I am a new lecturer in history at the new University of Malaya. The head of my department, Professor Cyril Northcote Parkinson, meets me as I come down the gang plank. So too am I welcomed by a tremendous cloud burst, thunder, lightning and torrents of tropical rain, "a Sumatra" so called.

As his syce drives us into town along Collyer Quay, skirting the crowded slum that is the town, round the *padang* and past the Shaw Building, Singapore's only high-rise, all of 16 floors, and then up languid Orchard Road to our leafy Tanglin campus well out of the crowded city, I seek some details from Parkinson as to my future. He gives cursory attention to this domestic chore — "world history with an Asian emphasis" is all I can gather. I gulp, then listen, as he launches into a survey of today's Asia, at once depressing and exciting. I give it to you 60 years later, the big picture as he painted it. It may help you to recall the environment created by the Cold War and the emergence of an independent Asia, in which I am to work for the next 14 years.

Inspired by the ideology of Karl Marx, the dynamism of Lenin and the example now of China but above all of Russia (which dominated the world-wide movement with its ruthless political, cultural and economic changes made on an unprecedented scale) revolutionary activists were striving, as they had for decades, to reach their goal of overthrowing the state and establishing a dictatorship of the proletariat. Singapore, stressed Parkinson, was not exempt from this.

Many businessmen in the city, so he told me, thought Singapore, with or without Malaya, would be the next to follow the Asian pattern. Nearly all the giant Chinese-language schools, which housed the majority of Singapore's young, had become Marxist-Maoist citadels of power. Nearly all the new trade unions were in similar thrall to the Party. The colonial regime was only weakly supported, and in any case as the British already had left India they could not be expected to remain in Singapore or Malaya much longer. He had no need to remind me that as far as the latter was concerned, a cruel war had been underway for over five years, with Chin Peng leading one of the most ruthless terrorist organisations in the world. There is little sign of it ending, he told me. A communist seizure of power in Singapore, Parkinson felt, must be considered a clear possibility.

Nor could Singapore — or the Malay Peninsula for that matter — ignore recent developments elsewhere in Asia. They were of a tectonic-plate magnitude. To our north a few years earlier, in 1948, China had collapsed to the communists led by Mao Tse Tung.

Of the refugees who had crowded into Hong Kong following the takeover a trickle still was coming south to Singapore, counter-balanced by the many Chinese who were leaving the island, returning home. Korea, divided after the Japanese surrender in August 1945 had been the scene of a major war when the communists came screaming south on June 25, 1950. An uneasy truce had been signed in June 1953, shortly before I arrived in Singapore. It could flare up again, Parkinson felt, at any time. He was less than happy also about developments in French Indo-China — or Vietnam as it was now being called. The French he felt were on the way out, the communists on the way in. And incidentally, did I know the Marine Police had rescued two French soldiers who had jumped overboard from the troopship I had seen that morning? Soon he felt the Vietminh as they were called would be close to northern Malaya (the debacle of Diem Bien Phu indeed was only a few months away). And to our south, he concluded, the world's largest communist party flexed its muscles as the nationalist demagogue Sukarno tried to balance his power base in the newly independent and unstable Indonesia.

Gloom and doom indeed. Of course I knew all this, I had lived with it, but then Parkinson struck a chord. I was not here merely to give a lecture program, he told me, far from it. Our graduates were required, urgently, to fill the gaps, and more, of the departing British civil servants, teachers, administrators, businessmen, all leaving Malaya and Singapore. Trained professionals in many walks of life were needed. It was essential that if Malaya and Singapore were to survive, let alone prosper, a solid middle class of indigenous citizens was needed; and fast. It did not matter if they were anti-colonial, indeed so much the better. What was essential was a backbone of anti-communism; or all was lost.

He enlarged on a characteristic of all Colonies, worldwide, a lack of self-confidence. The Colonial Master, the *"Tuan"*, was always the leader; he made all the decisions, while generation after generation of local people had it so drilled into them that they were inferior and incompetent that they believed it themselves.

We had to conquer this all pervasive assumption if we were ever to help in the creation of a nation. Essentially we are here, he said, you and I and all others on this campus, not to perpetuate the past but to participate in the future.

By this time we are sweeping up the drive that I later learn circles the pre-war Raffles College, the site of the university. Parkinson's office is on the first floor over an archway through which in a month's time undergraduates will stream, heading for their canteen. With greenery all around the hill top is charming.

Upstairs my colleagues are called from their rooms by Mat the departmental peon or office boy. I am introduced to them one by one. Mat hovers, so I extend my hand to him too. I had learned on the ship the Malay greeting, so bravely I say "selamat pagi" (good morning). Surprised, he gives me the soft handshake which I had been told was the custom. He is to be my friend for life, and will be at the wharf to farewell me, 14 years later.

I soon discover I had joined a team of quality academics. Alas, they did not stay for long. Eric Stokes would write several highly acclaimed books on India before occupying the prestigious Jan Smuts Chair of Commonwealth History at Cambridge. Graham Irwin — with someone else's wife — there was a lot of that in the expatriate community — would be headhunted by Columbia University in New York. David Bassett would become head of Hull's centre for Southeast Asian Studies. Len Young would move to a chair at Hong Kong. Ian McGregor would go as professor to Ghana, to its new university.

Fortunately, they would be replaced by other eager beavers, locally domiciled, high quality graduates all with overseas qualifications, the earliest of whom, Wang Gungwu, is there to meet me. When Parkinson left some years later I was to play a part in their graduate advance and placement, indeed to work myself out of a job. But expatriate as it then was, local as it became, it was a most stimulating environment, with other Faculties reflecting our eagerness to make the university an institution that would win world recognition and of which Singapore and Malaya could be proud.

2 The Campus

In those early years the communist menace that Parkinson had outlined had a prominence, a reality, difficult today to imagine. Sixty years on the brutality of it all, the terrible wrongs and terrors inflicted on innocent individuals by this worldwide revolutionary movement are forgotten or ignored, as they were then by many academics, while the cause itself has vanished almost without trace, even from Russia and China. Yet at the time, as Parkinson said, "we could be the next to go".

I had little fear that this would be, provided that those in Singapore who were opposed to it acted. Yet I could not understand how so many were dedicated believers of this foul cause. Back in Australia, a fairy land of ignorance, I had academic friends — Dorothy Hewett the playwright, the historians Russel Ward and Manning Clark ("the communist Party is the conscience of Australia", he once said), the author-lawyer Lloyd Davies among them — all committed communists. They, I felt, were part of a lunatic Left, remote from reality. But here, in the frontline as it were, it was even more unbelievable. How could this be, I wondered.

So I sought enlightenment from my new campus colleagues, particularly Ungku Abdul Aziz, a Malay aristocrat in the Economics Department, and Wang Gungwu, a fellow historian. Surely no one could possibly envy China or Russia with their communes, collective farms and discredited economic practices? Surely the individualistic Chinese who crowded the roadside Five Foot Ways doing business in the open, each one endeavouring to climb the ladder of economic success, could not embrace the totality of state control of all their enterprises? So what's in it for them — or the Malay peasant working his padi field or tapping his rubber small holding?

You have it all wrong I was told, it's not economics but politics.

Lenin and Mao supplied an organisational answer to the problems of political authority of particular relevance to Colonies. Here was a proven formula for social mobilisation as well as a justification for political power, and an effective means for harnessing the resentment against Western dominance. Maoism (and Marxism) must be seen as a political answer, not economic, to explain its acceptance by so many.

All this applied more to Singapore and the Chinese in general than to the Malays where, Ungku Abdul Aziz said, their faith and semi-feudal system inhibited them from radicalism of most kinds. Indeed, he said, he saw communalism, that is the ongoing relationship with the Chinese, as far more of a permanent weakness to the peninsula than communism, despite the war being fought there. However, Gungwu added, another factor to explain the strength of the communist movement on the island was the centuries old Chinese tradition, very much alive, of secret society involvement in clandestine revolutionary activity. He spoke with some authority, as his research thesis on Chinese Revolutionaries in Singapore and Penang, 1900–1911, had earned him a First Class Honours degree only a few months earlier.

Gungwu was heading for a distinguished academic career of international repute. He was respected even then by his peers and elders for his level headedness and impartial assessment of contemporary affairs, rare for one so young. He accepted the success of the Communists in attacking the widespread grievances of the proletariat, ignored by the colonialists, but he pointed to their failure to commit themselves in any meaningful way to the Malayan nation-building process. "This is their Achilles heel," he said. "The sooner Malaya is a state the better. Singapore too. Capitalism inside a nation-state will defeat communism any time."

I retained my doubts. Watching the fire storm in nearby Vietnam, seeing the communist success in Korea and China, anticipating a coup in Indonesia, most of Malaya communist controlled, I could not be that confident that all would be well. Nevertheless when 40 years later, Gungwu, by then an elder statesman among academics, was to say much the same to the MCP leader Chin Peng, what was the latter's reply? "I agree with you."

Another who was anxious to participate in the nation building process was Lee Kuan Yew, a young Singapore lawyer. He had no time for the Old Hong Kong cliché that justified the perpetuation of Colonial rule — "the Chinese do not care who holds the cow, provided they can milk it" — nor for the many who, as a fellow member of the Royal Singapore Yacht Club put it, "there's no problem here that a good division of British Troops could not solve". He could see a third path leading to a non-communist anti-colonial independent country, and he set out to rally support for such an ideal.

In 1954, during my first academic year, he formed the People's Action Party with that purpose in mind. While many in the city and on the campus regarded it as so far to the Left as to be almost undistinguishable from the communists, and were wary of this young lawyer's rhetoric, I felt he was the hope of the future. In fact it was to be touch and go. Between 1956–58 in particular, he and his team of English-educated middle class cohorts were riding a tiger. In those years, 1956 and 1957 in particular the PAP was a virtual prisoner of the communists who in 1957 mounted a nearly successful attempt to capture its executive committee. It took a decade of dedicated drive for him to prevail, only to have his cup of success dashed from his lips, and then again to succeed.

Our campus only a decade earlier had been General Tomoyuki Yamashita's headquarters, alongside the Botanical Gardens then being administered by Count Yoshichika Tokugawa, the son of Japan's last shogun. History was all around it, and in the local staff in particular who lectured there. It was no ivory tower, rather a ferment of conflicting views as to the evolution of Singapore.

Some were politically apathetic, cushioned by colonialism for too long. Lee Kuan Yew described them as "effete time servers, the English-educated intelligentsia". Others, a few, were dedicated communists, while many were apprehensive and uncertain as to what to do.

At a cheerful gathering for my first-year students (they came in those days from all over Malaya), I talked amongst others with Sally Ong from Penang. A few days later her absence from a tutorial was excused by another Malayan. Her father, a well-known medico, had been called out to an alleged emergency. He was shot and killed by the communist unit then based in Georgetown, with others in the island's interior. The Ongs had been in Penang for generations, part of the "Queens Chinese" as they were known, loyal subjects that were staunchly opposed to the communists. This was the response.

The communists were hunted with some success, but by 1959 there was still a hard core, possibly some thirty, either in Georgetown itself or in the valleys and jungle behind. They were smuggled out, so we heard later, on Chin Peng's orders, some across the straits to Acheh, others to the Perak interior, the *ulu*, deep in the forest.

Dr Ong's murder was in Penang. We had worries enough closer to our campus. In May that year (1954) occurred the Hock Lee bus riots. Mobs of over 2,000 Chinese-language students and other communist supporters stormed the streets of Chinatown, attacked the police and inflicted much damage as for several days, they virtually controlled the city. David Marshall's government regained control with difficulty.

Near our Raffles College campus was the Chinese High School. We watched with some apprehension as trucks packed with its students surged past, roaring "patriotic" songs, clenched fists held high as they headed into town. Another stream on foot crowded Bukit Timah Road. One of my colleagues, Patrick de Joselyn de Jong, was caught on his way out of the campus. His car was overturned and torched, he, badly shaken, scrambled to the safety

9

of our nearby home. Others were not so fortunate. Three were killed. It was a disturbing scene.

Another first-year student who was our guest that evening was Edwin Thumboo. He was arrested in May 1954 on the day when he and six other undergraduates, members of the university Socialist Party, were due to sit their end of year examinations. They were charged with sedition. This was at a time when agreement had been reached by the various European powers involved to bring about a peaceful settlement in Korea and Indochina. Another conference in Europe, this time at Geneva, saw an end to hostilities — although it proved temporary as far as Vietnam was concerned. Thumboo's crime was to criticise the still dominant role of Europeans in the affairs of Asia, and the exclusion of an Asian voice. The formation of SEATO (South East Asian Treaty Organisation) in September that year, "a military pact in Asia without Asian participation" gave emphasis to his point. "The time is past," he wrote, "When European nations could make decisions binding on Asia."

Fajar, the student newspaper, had an influence beyond the campus, but nevertheless as a one time editor of an undergraduate rag myself, I thought it fairly innocuous, and the reactions of the Colonial government extreme. I had my class stand for a moment in sympathy.

The Vice-chancellor, Sir Sydney Caine, summoned me to his office shortly after. He had little sympathy for the young who ventured opinions of this sort, or for those Asians critical of Europeans who governed them. Nor was there much support for lecturers who encouraged it. Hong Kong, he reminisced happily, handled this sort of nonsense much better. I was advised to watch it.

I visited Thumboo, cheered at his trial in August, heard Lee Kuan Yew demolish the prosecution, and welcomed Thumboo back to the campus. In time he became emeritus professor of English on that campus, with an international reputation as a poet. Our long lasting friendship was marked by a large cake and a warm hug at a reunion on the campus for my 80th birthday in June 2003.

I had judged correctly that Thumboo and his friends were not communists, but I erred markedly in my encouragement of another student, a Sikh named Jamit Singh. We often met in the nearby Botanical Gardens where sometimes he took my place pushing the pram of my baby daughter. He had abandoned the outward signs of his faith, the turban, the comb, the iron bracelet, had cut his hair and drastically trimmed his beard to little more than stubble. He was strangely lonely and on the point of abandoning the campus as well. I tried to dissuade him, to no avail. He had a deep hatred of the injustices of Colonialism, of how in Singapore in all walks of official life the local was treated as second rate, inferior. Pay, leave, other conditions of work, housing — all was biased against him. He told me of the deplorable slums that housed the mainly Tamil wharf labourers. He was going to do something about it. I rather weakly argued that the government was doing what it could, but Singapore was a free port, there was no revenue there, no chance of an effective income tax, before the war the island's revenue had come largely from a controlled sale of opium and a license to gamble, both now dubbed "Yellow Culture". Jamit was not impressed. He quit the campus and as secretary of the Harbour Board Staff Association became one of the "Big Six" union leaders, all pro-communist. He achieved great notoriety as an outspoken, virulent speaker, but after being detained for some time his influence faded. Nevertheless, the conditions of the wharf labourers improved considerably.

Maurice Baker's room was down the corridor from mine. We shared morning tea together. He was a lecturer in English, and had been a quiet member of Lee Kuan Yew's group since student days in London. He asked me to take on a Malay Studies honours student named Linda Chen. The entire Malay Studies Department was moving to the new university outside Kuala Lumpur. Linda was banned from entering the peninsula as her earlier involvement with the Singapore Middle School Students Union made her totally unacceptable to a country at war with the communists. She had rare assets, fluent and literate in Malay, English, Hokkien

11

and Mandarin. The PAP wanted to keep an eye on her, not have her vanish into the underground. She was an excellent student and a charming person. Her master's thesis, on the early newspapers of Singapore, I subsequently had published. But shortly after she had presented it to me she was arrested.

"Also Held: Linda Chen and Sister" was the headline in the February 3, 1963 *Straits Times*, which told of 107 arrests as part of Operation Cold Store. A Left-wing revolt in Brunei, Sukarno pushing troops into Sarawak, Sabah and Johor, explosions in downtown Singapore, plans to assassinate Mr Lee who was being violently abused in Malaya, strong island support for the open front Barisan Socialist Party, all threatened the island's future. Much later I was told by George Bogaars, head of the Special Branch and a good friend, that Linda had been in contact with Chin Peng, and while I had naïvely thought I was merely encouraging a gifted academic she was actively building up a cell on the campus. Mao Tse Tung had begun his career in a like manner.

After she was released from internment, by then totally disillusioned by the falsity of communism, I helped her enrol in Liverpool University, and corresponded with her when she returned to Singapore. She opened a bookshop, but had a rotten time of it from the authorities. She died, aged 74, in 2003.

And there were other, if not communists then agents of one kind or another working for their government while using their academic qualifications and background as a cloak to hide their basic reason for being on our campus. An Israeli "scholar", Moshe Yegar, who I had helped in various ways, was later expelled from Malaya, an Australian (Mervyn Jaspan), a visiting "scholar" from Taiwan, various Americans, I doubt if they did much damage, if any, but we became suspicious of them all. Even Parkinson.

He had a regular gathering of senior students at his home, where a VIP of one sort or another would talk and answer questions. Academically sound and non-controversial; yet next morning, his secretary would type a lengthy account of it and send it to the British High Commission.

I ventured into the VIP business myself, with an unexpected result. At the time I was lecturing on modern Southeast Asia, and to give the poor students some respite from the droning of a thick Australian accent, I organised a series of talks, one a week, of visitors invited to speak on their role in their nation's move to independence. They went so well that I introduced our last speaker to what had become a crowded lecture theatre.

G. Djatikusomo was Indonesia's Consul General in Singapore. He was also a General of the Indonesian army, and on its role against the Dutch he spoke with fervour. With blackboard and chalk to help he outmanoeuvred them, cut behind them, attacked their flank, managed victory it appeared even when retreating, while as far as we could gather, Sukarno was watching *wayang* theatre in Soerabaja. He spoke with passion as he relived those critical years, making specific reference to the hopes entertained at the Japanese-sponsored meeting of Sukarno and Hatta in August 1945 with Malay left wing leaders in Ipoh. Here the concept of a Republic of Greater Indonesia was accepted. It was to include all of the Dutch East Indies, the Malay Peninsula, Timor and all Borneo. Sultanates would be abolished and Batavia, renamed Djakarta, would be the capital of this new Republic. The vehemence in which this dream was relived made us uncomfortable. We stirred in our seats.

He turned to look at me, not a friendly glance, but more a glare, as he then attacked the British for sending troops into Java in 1946, and proclaimed that the wicked intrigues of the Western Imperialists and their running dogs of supporters would never prevail. "No job for you, Tuan", he said. It was an unexpected demonstration of rudeness so unlike the courtesy one had come to appreciate from all my Malay friends, for indeed it was endemic to their culture.

Neither the concept of Malaya becoming a minor part of a Republic of Indonesia nor the personal slight to me went down well. Feet were shuffled, two students walked out to a hush of astonishment. His assistant, Raden Wongsodidjojo, whispered to him. He concluded his talk to desultory clapping. A great pity, for it had been a most interesting insight into recent events that had helped shape the region.

I heard later that Djatikusomo had been recruiting Left-wing activists in Singapore on the understanding they would help liberate Irian Jaya from the Dutch. Actually these naïve youngsters were sent offshore to the Rhio Archipelago. Here they were trained to infiltrate back into Singapore. In this they failed dismally.

We were amused to hear some years later that, as Indonesia's ambassador in Kuala Lumpur, he had become lost for several days in Kedah's *ulu* near Haadyai while trying to renew contact with Chin Peng, then in South Thailand. Or perhaps the Special Branch, charged with tagging him, lost contact; whatever, it illustrates the underhand activities of a so-called diplomat, and as far as I was concerned, that ended my program of VIP's.

It may have played some part, however, in a later invitation to represent Singapore at a small UN conference on the role of the working class in the national struggle for independence. Some 40 delegates, French or English-speakers, nearly all ethnic citizens of former African or Asian colonies, were the guests of Habib Bourgiba, President of Tunisia. He gave us a magnificent reception at his villa at Sidi Bou Said, overlooking the Mediterranean, not far from the ruins of ancient Carthage.

I apologise for taking you a long way from Singapore and its university but please stay with me, for the tale I tell is not merely relevant to the history of that area but to the future of all of us, wherever we may be.

The President was asked what or who had inspired him to fight the French for independence. Nationalist leaders in British colonies could look back on George Washington and other success stories in British history for several centuries following. There was a clear pattern of imperial withdrawal. India the most recent. But where, I asked, was the French precedent, what inspired someone in a French environment, where assimilation, not independence, was the goal?

Bourgiba had the magnificent black eyes of a Berber. They flashed as he glared at me, spitting out "assimilation" in disgust. He sketched in his background. He told how when he was a boy in Monastir, the coastal town venerated by the Tunisians (Moslem to a man), French legionaries would use the walls of the mosque for the public execution of the many Tunisian revolutionaries condemned to death. He recalled an incident of equal blindness when the French actually celebrated the success of one of the Crusades by staging an elaborate procession on its anniversary, dressing up in Crusader costumes and forcing many school boys — himself among them — to participate in a grand parade of Christian triumph. He went on to list other slights, most of them religiously based. Clearly the thrust of French colonialism, to make all citizens French in culture and become integral parts of France, had been heavy-handed and maladroit. And in his drive for independence, he told us, he looked for inspiration above all not to France but to the patriot rebels in Catholic Ireland. "Oh the blindness of the British", he said. The French-speaking contingent, nearly all of them African, burst into applause.

My Russian companion, V.G. Troukhanovsky from the USSR Academy of Science in Moscow, was puzzled. "Marx said 'religion is the opiate of the people'. It makes them accept life, not rebel", he said. He could not understand the role religion played in stimulating the national feelings of this leader, or any other. With S.V. Kodikara of Ceylon (Sri Lanka) and Raychaudhuri of the Delhi School of Economics helping we endeavoured to explain it to him. For indeed to Asian nationalists it was very familiar.

In Burma it had been the Young Men's Buddhist Association, formed in 1906, that first brought together those opposing the British. A reviving Islam had sparked major opposition to the Dutch in Indonesia with the formation of Sarekat Islam in 1912. In Thailand, Buddhism had been a major element in traditional culture that helped maintain the country's independence, while in Malaya, where we were witnessing the emergence of a new nation, Islam again was a factor of national strength. Moslem opposition in the Southern Philippines had opposed Catholic Manila with success. Pakistan came into existence mainly due to Islam.

All this we explained to Troukhanovsky as we headed south on a five-day tour of Tunisia. Turkish coastal forts gave way to a Roman aqueduct stretching for over 30 kilometres to the ruins of Thuburbo Majus, sacked by the Vandals. Over rolling plains, once the granary of Rome, not a tree, not a fence, with nomadic Berbers, sheep and camels, to Kairouan, the oldest Arab city in all Africa. In its magnificent mosque we were shown the Roman pillars brought there by Christian prisoners in the 9th century. Then the immense coliseum of El Djem and finally, far to the south, the lovely oasis of Nefta. Gazing over the desert, eating dates, our Russian friend watched as, with the sun setting over the Sahara, the whole oasis stopped and, as if on a parade ground rather than the courtyard of a mosque, turned towards Mecca and prayed. "Now I understand", he said.

So must all of us; for today 50 years on the militant Moslem, with the courtyard of his mosque the inviolate parade ground of Islam, is not now merely of academic interest relevant only to the history of former Colonies of the West but is assertive world-wide. Particularly in all countries where a critical mass of Moslem minorities refuse to integrate, a danger grows to endanger the stability of these countries. In Western Asia, over which I flew while returning to Singapore, its legacy is turmoil.

After ten days in Tunisia it was difficult to return to Singapore but soon the routine of academic life, of lectures and tutorials with hardworking students absorbed me once again. And since "Campus" heads this chapter, let me conclude as I began, with a campus episode concerning Parkinson.

He had set his sights on becoming Dean of the Arts Faculty. In an effort to obtain sufficient votes for this exalted position he asked me — no, told me — to secure the support for his nomination from K.C. Ho, head of the Chinese Department, a staunch traditionalist. I was not happy about this, for to send an underling to seek a favour from a mandarin is just not on. I knew enough about Chinese etiquette to understand that I was provoking a totally unproductive loss of face. In any case, if we were preparing for the future, should we not assist Asians into positions of power, rather than retain them ourselves? However, along I went.

My fears were confirmed. As Mr Ho, in his formal Confucian gown pointed out, Parkinson had not done him the honour of approaching him personally, and to deal with a mere lecturer, so he intimated with quite unnecessary subtlety, was less than satisfactory. He regretted he could not support such a proposal.

Generously he threw me a life line. Had I mistaken my mission, was it Mr Ho of the Geography Department I should see? No, I knew Bobby Ho, he sailed with me, his English wife was our friend too. "Oh, do you sail a junk?" asked my Confucian colleague. He was not really part of modern, egalitarian Singapore; but he had been part of Australia. So to conclude the interview I asked him had he enjoyed his time in Canberra, at the Australian National University. "It was not all to our liking," he said. "Conditions were terrible. There were no servants and" — he drew himself up in horror — "do you know, my wife had to chop the wood?" I shared his horror, and bowing deeply, retreated, walking backwards to the door.

Parkinson was never Dean of Arts. Rather he incorporated my experience in an article he sent off to the English *Economist*. This, along with several later submissions, was published as *Parkinson's Law* ("work expands to fill the time available"). The book was a sensation. It became a best seller. He achieved worldwide recognition as a critical satirist of socialist bureaucracy. He resigned while on long service leave to enjoy a life of fortune and fame. I succeeded him as, somewhat to my surprise, I became in 1959 the last Raffles Professor of History on that campus.

3 Merdeka

"Merdeka; Merdeka", they shouted, a group of youngsters waving and running happily beside us as our university mini bus drove into their *kampong*. Kota Kuala Muda — fort at the mouth of the Muda River — was its name, and once it had guarded Kedah's southern regions. There were the remains of a brick wall to prove it. But in fact it was no more than a small collection of Malay huts on stilts haphazardly scattered under Casuarina trees, a row of wooden Chinese shop houses, and a small mosque. Here the boys who had welcomed us with their cheerful cry of "freedom" helped us with our *barang* (luggage) and crowded round as we saluted with a soft handshake their religious leader, the *kathi*, and my host, Haji Ahmad. So began one of my most enjoyable weeks in Malaya.

By now (January 1955) the war in Malaya was winding down. But as one student, Mohammed Khalil, wrote long after, "In Malaya in 1954 it was still a time of uncertainty and uneasiness as the war waged by the communist terrorists (the CTs) was still going on unabated. I remember the train taking us to Singapore to the university left Kuala Lumpur at ten at night and arrived in Singapore about eight the next morning. Throughout the night just a few hundred yards ahead of the locomotive there was an armoured car leading the way to check whether the line had been tampered with or to take the brunt of any explosion from a landmine which might have been placed there. A disturbing start to an academic year."

"Just over a year earlier two young Malays who I knew from Kampong Tasik (just six miles from Ipoh) died in a hail of sten gun bullets as they cycled home along the railway track one night as they refused to surrender their identity cards when stopped by the CTs. Earlier, in 1948 when at school, there was another hail of sten gun bullets from CTs directed at a group of Orang Asli who were having their photographs taken near us for their identity cards. We scrambled out of the classroom to find safety in the school lavatory, which had brick walls."

"In 1954, when our group went to university, communists were in power in China, and closer to us, the French had been defeated at Diem Bien Phu. Communism seemed poised to take over the world. General Templer had come in 1952 and maybe the 'ism' was being contained, but for how long? And meanwhile up and down the peninsula innocent Asian throats were being cut, bellies of pregnant women disembowelled, and tappers (and planters) shot without mercy", wrote Mohammed Khalil.

General Sir Gerald Templer, the battalions of British troops and their increasingly effective tactics in jungle warfare, the resettlement of thousands of Chinese squatters from the jungle edges to protected "new villages", and the gradual strengthening of political and practical support by all the races of Malaya, given the prospect of imminent independence, turned the tide. Alas, the lessons learned here were judged irrelevant in Vietnam, where a decade or more of failed war saw the communists eventually triumph.

I had become more and more interested in the history of early Southeast Asia and was attempting to lecture on it. Although the Malay Peninsula itself had never been the centre of any great Asian civilisation, it certainly had been involved in those that had flourished nearby on Java and Sumatra in the first or early in the second millennia. Clearly there was no vast temple complex waiting to be discovered but surely some legacy of the millennia might still remain? But was it safe to look?

Most of Johor, that part of the peninsula nearest to Singapore, was Black, controlled by CTs. Yong Peng for example, which straddled the main trunk road to Kuala Lumpur was a district to be avoided until the late 1950s. Hoi Lung, the MCP leader, was a feared and brutal man. So too his organisation, replenished regularly from Singapore. When in August 1958 Dato Abdul Razak, the Defence Minister of the newly independent Malaya, visited the village to announce the lifting of all restrictions following Hoi Lung's defection, and so making it White, only 100 of the 6,300 Chinese villagers turned out to hear him. Their surly hatred of Government was deep. Driving through it on the way to Kuala Lumpur always gave you an uneasy feeling.

Kulai was another hard core communist district in South Johor. Further north, all Pahang was out of bounds for many years except to the military, and so too the Sungei Siput district in Perak. This had been Chin Peng's stamping ground in the years of Japanese occupation and it was here that a series of murders instigated the Emergency in 1948. It remained a fanatically hostile communist area until 1958 at least.

Elsewhere, however, there was by 1954, an increasing level of law and order. It began in Malacca, the ancient settlement — Malay, Portuguese, Dutch, British — where the lack of incidents of terror and the preponderance of Malays and anti-Communist Chinese (led by Tan Cheng Lock — whose biography I later wrote) enabled Templer in late 1953, shortly after we arrived, to lift all Emergency Regulations, declaring it White. Local government functioned again, people and goods moved freely and its historic bullock carts, *Kereta Lembu*, lumbered along sleepy lanes, now untroubled by communist terrorists. Other areas elsewhere in Malaya followed, including south Kedah, near Penang.

It was this area that interested us when we formed in 1954 the university archaeological society. Miscellaneous discoveries outlined by H.G. Quaritch-Wales in pre-war issues of the *Journal of the Malayan branch of the Royal Asiatic Society* (JMBRAS) suggested it could have been the site of an early Indian-influenced settlement. With fellow enthusiasts, particularly Paul Wheatley, a geographer later to be headhunted by the University of Chicago, we decided to go look. But first we had better know what we were looking for. So we arranged a course of instruction on Buddhist art at the national museum in Bangkok.

Our journey there was not without incident. Travelling with Wheatley in an old Land Rover, we broke down on a lonely stretch of the main road in north Johor. Wheatley thumbed a lift to obtain help from the next village. I sat in the Land Rover and waited. The view was not exciting; rubber trees by the thousand on one side of the road, the jungle on the other. It was late afternoon; long shadows were creeping towards us. Although the trees and the undergrowth, the *lalang*, had been cut back from the road to make ambushes more difficult, it was still less than an appealing prospect. I suddenly realised the green coloured Land Rover had a vaguely military air. The thought did little to comfort me.

Suddenly out of nowhere a face appeared at the car window. Startled, I realised it was that of a Malay boy. I wiped the sweat from my brow and, smiling at him for sympathy, said, *"panas"* (hot) with some feeling. He looked at me impassively. I had a thought. Holding up my empty thermos flask I queried *"ayer?"* (water?). He nodded, took it and vanished. The shadows crept closer. It was utterly still, and heavy with heat. Where the hell was Wheatley? Then again the face appeared, with the thermos flask, "Thank you thank you", I said in Malay. Where was his kampong, I wondered, as I unscrewed the top, more than ready for a cool drink. It was filled with hot water.

Wheatley arrived with a Chinese mechanic, the car was soon started and we reached Seremban before dark. At a roadside mobile drinks stall, a *warong minuman*, I drank for the first time the deliciously cool *air batu manis*, water with syrup and flaked ice. The next day we drove uneventfully the length of the peninsula to Butterworth on the Straits of Malacca and crossed by the car ferry to historic Penang, passing close to a moored P&O (Peninsular and Oriental Steam Navigation Company) passenger liner on the way.

We stayed that night at the Eastern and Oriental Hotel, the "E&O" as generations of travellers and Malayan hands knew it. Built in 1884 by the Sarkies Brothers, it rivalled in renown the

Raffles of Singapore. If by 1954 it was somewhat rundown, as was Penang itself, its languid charm nevertheless was captivating. The ancient elevator laboured to lift me up to the third floor, a creaking and rattling cage. Somerset Maughan and Noel Coward must have used the same lift. Conrad probably just preceded it.

The hotel stands close to the sea, and when the Malay "boy" threw open the old wooden shutters, the room was filled with the gentle splash of the tide against the seawall. A junk sailed slowly across, a rising full moon was framed by two palm trees and from my private balcony I glimpsed the massive bulk of Gunong Jerai on the coast of Kedah. Nearby the ruins of Fort Cornwallis took me back to Francis Light and the settlement's foundations in 1786. Behind me was *Bukit Bendera*, Penang Hill, a landfall feature for centuries along with Gunong Jerai for sailors far out to sea. The next day, joined by eight undergraduates, we caught the train to Bangkok.

All morning we chugged across the emerald green padi fields of Kedah dotted by docile water buffalo, *kerbau*, pulling their single-furrow plough. Nothing could have been more peaceful. Cool air, undisturbed by so much as a raised voice, rushed down our half empty second-class Pullman carriage, one of several tacked on behind a sleeper and a dining car. I enjoyed talking to my students or reading or admiring Malaya's rice bowl.

One such student who remained my friend until his death a few years ago was Joginder Singh Jessy, author of a textbook on Malaysian history that was for a time widely used in Malaysian schools. He was almost my age, but the war had interrupted his education, as it had mine. All of us called him "uncle Joe". He was always borrowing or lending money. He had joined the Indian National Army, was one of those, so he told me, who in September 1943 had paraded on the *padang* before Tojo, the Japanese Prime Minister. He had enlisted, so he maintained, only to get two meals a day. He spent 1944 in Bangkok while watching the I.N.A. disintegrate before the British advance. He realised he had backed the wrong horse.

He had a rubber smallholding in upper Kedah, but it was worked by a relative while he taught in a primary school in Penang — which he had visited the previous morning. Now he was firmly committed to an independent Malaya, and felt it essential the communist killers be eliminated. He had some personal reasons for this, as his small holding was near Haadyai, the border village a few miles ahead. In 1949 it had been burnt down by the same MCP unit that had murdered the rubber planters and their tappers in Sungei Siput the previous year. For all he knew it was still around. He added, "They burnt the train as well." I shifted uncomfortably in my seat; but all went well.

(Haadyai, incidentally, was to be the place where Chin Peng concluded secret negotiations begun in Phuket and — returning from his Chinese sanctuary — signed on 8 December 1989 the Peace Agreement whereby the MCP laid down its arms to end the Emergency.)

Unknown to us, a world-title feather weight boxing match was being staged in Bangkok. Once we had passed Haadyai, and had been photographed at the border, each stopping place in South Thailand was packed with people determined to journey on our train. The Thai defender in the boxing match was a serving policeman. Every police station in Thailand sold tickets, and if you knew what was good for you, you bought one.

All afternoon and most of the night they poured on board, and carriage after carriage was added. Somewhere in the evening, around 3 a.m., I woke from a fitful doze as we drew into another village. By now the half empty carriage was long gone, and so was the Anglo-Saxon-Malay restraint, the quiet and good order. In its place was an excited voluble mob of scores of people and their belongings, surging into an already packed carriage. I was jammed into a corner with a large Thai next to me, his friend sitting on the arm of the seat, others around my feet, with the aisle of the Pullman jammed two deep. Somehow as well innumerable wicker baskets were packed in, most carrying fruits for peddling in Bangkok.

My Malayan friends came swinging down the racks, the only way to travel, and initiated me into haggling for and then consuming some rather strange-looking pieces of refreshment being hawked outside. Full of good cheer, the crowded carriage watched and applauded as I concluded the transaction. The din was terrific, a full volumed exchange of shouting, haggling, laughing, from and between the outside crowd and the packed carriage.

With dawn and much laughter as unconcernedly they jockeyed for precarious positions to carry out the most intimate stages of their toilet, nearly all clutching hand-bowls, many beautifully made in traditional patterns, which were used as a wash basin, a food container and much else. In this I joined them, given a bowl with some water by Krishnan Iyer, a student, while Joginder Singh guarded my seat. His smattering of war-time Thai and his fierce bearded appearance saved it for me. With him and the others I shared some delicious *pisang mas* bananas and some water.

Toilet and breakfast over, the carriage in good humour settled down somewhat as heavy rain forced shut all the windows. They were still shut and the air carried a most ghastly odour when at 1 p.m. we reached Bangkok; or rather the broad Chao Phraya River, with Thailand's capital on the other bank. We crossed by a dilapidated ferry, giving us a view downstream of the towering Wat Arun.

Siam, recently renamed Thailand was not in my good books. During the war it had helped itself to a large part of western Cambodia, the French being impotent to stop it, and later in October 1943 it re-asserted its ancient authority over the northern Malay States of Perlis, Kedah, Kelantan and Trengganu. This availed it nothing when war ended but to me and many others it left a bitter taste of political opportunism. However, Bangkok was a new experience, all of it good.

Bangkok in 1954 was a small town, crisscrossed by *klongs*, sluggish canals creeping towards the river, where bred immense hungry mosquitoes. Long since drained and replaced with arterial roads, they represented just one aspect of an earlier era. So too the pre-war river bank Oriental Hotel, one of the few hotels in the city. Not a high-rise office block in sight, and few enough cars.

One such *klong*, cluttered with slow moving filth, drifted past the Chinese YMCA on Sathon Road on the outskirts of town, where we stayed. There were large vents in my mosquito net. The meals, largely dry fish, rice, soft fried egg and floppy bread, were difficult to handle with chopsticks.

The national museum, totally unaware of tourists of any kind, nevertheless did us proud with a course in Buddhist art. We were shown illustrations of the Eight Great Events in the life of Buddha, and taught the meaning of the various gestures of his right hand, as shown on numerous statues — teaching, fearlessness, reassurance, bestowing a blessing, meditation, amongst others. We studied the differing cranial bumps on his head of great significance in all dating of statues, and the cultural periods to which they belonged. Lopburi, Sukothai, Pracchinburi, Dvaravati and Ayutthaya as well as Bangkok were thrown at us in various tests. In this Paul Wheatley excelled. Indeed I felt this erudite scholar knew more than our museum instructor. It little mattered. None of what we learned here, interesting as it was had any relevance, so we learned later, to our subsequent expedition in Kedah. A course in Hindu art would have been more relevant.

One afternoon Dean Rong Syamanda of Chulalongkorn University (who became a lifelong friend) with a group of his students took us all up the Chao Phraya to Ayutthaya, the ruined capital sacked by the Burmese in the 1760s. We had a delightful picnic exploring the ruins. It was a new thing for Asian students to meet and the event caused great excitement. The *Bangkok Post* gave us quite a spread, naming us all. I suppose we spoke nearly a dozen languages. We conversed, of course, in English.

One Thai undergraduate was an attractive member of the royal family. On a later occasion she took us through the royal palace complex to areas not usually open to outsiders. Here in large glass cases were several *bungamas* (flowers of gold) sent in tribute from outlying fiefdoms. The largest, some six feet high, were from Chiang Mai, in the north; but those from the Malay states of Kedah, Kelantan and Trengganu, although diminutive in comparison, left no doubt as to where 19th-century overlordship lay. The tribute practice continued, for Kedah and Kelantan at least, every three years until the early 20th century. The last *bungamas* arrived in Bangkok in 1909, in time to be despatched to London as a coronation gift to King George V. Presumably then the last gold flowers of Kedah now repose in Windsor Castle, where possibly the subtlety of the gift may be appreciated.

The Chulalongkorn students organised a great dinner of Thai delicacies where we watched some beautiful classical dancing. We also visited the Hen Lak Hung, the biggest opium den in the world. On its four floors it had 5,000 permanent lodgers. Perhaps 1,000 more came each night. It was a vast building like a huge covered sheep pen, divided into low cubicles, each timbered (teak) to waist height, wire-partitioned above. Each cubicle held two or three reclining smokers, lying on their sides, their heads resting on a shaped teak pillow, a pipe to their lips. Hundreds more, naked above the loin cloth, peacefully wandered the aisles. Some were playing mahjong. We were shown around by Chee Fook, the manager. His impassivity was broken momentarily when he realised one of his guests was a girl, Mavis Scharenguivel, possibly the first woman ever to be there.

Mavis was to marry James Puthucheary, one of the leading lights in the small English-educated Marxist group. He never became a communist himself but he accepted virtually all of the Third International's manifesto for the overthrow of the capitalist state, and for this reason spent several years interned on St. Johns Island. I knew him slightly and had several stimulating discussions with him and fellow Economics Department students. He wrote a most interesting and controversial book entitled *Ownership and Control in the Malayan Economy*, which Donald Moore published in 1960. It reflected his extreme anti-capitalist and anti-colonial leanings. Come Singapore's independence he was banished from the island. Ironically enough, a successful legal career in Kuala

Lumpur was to follow. We often wondered, years after this trip to Bangkok, whether Mavis was some form of courier for the Party. In or out of opium dens, I found her charming.

Opium dens, the Western name conveying a sense of oriental depravity, were in fact working men's clubs. They served a social purpose. A poor devil whose day had been spent pedalling a heavy pedicab, or humping loads on the dockside with stomach muscles in agony, would obtain relief, even a drugged happiness, after a few pipes at the Hen Lak Hung or any other of the 100 smaller "dens" then licensed. In 1959 following overseas criticism and condemnation, the government thought it necessary to close them down. Making the drug illegal was not really the answer. As with Prohibition in the USA, it did not work. Both countries forgot that laws always should reflect social needs, not moral repugnance.

A year later we were in another world, much simpler and attuned to the enduring flow of nature, when we drove into kampong Kota Kuala Muda on the Kedah coast. A Malay kampong has a self-sufficiency in tune with the land and the spirit of the earth that those who live there — or even temporary visitors such as our archaeological student group — absorb with ease. It is understandable that the intellectual spirit, the related ideas of individuality and achievement brought by the West finds little expression in such an environment. In its place is peace and acceptance.

This was not so a few years earlier. Mohd. Akib bin Yaacob, the district officer, raised his hands in horror as he told me that as late as 1951–52 "this was a bandit infested area, a real black spot", and often in the dead of night the frantic beating of the mosque drum alerted all, including a nearby British army unit to another CT raid from their nearby mountain refuge. Now however, all was at peace, and little children ran before us waving and shouting "Merdeka" (freedom) without a worry in the world.

The *kathi* gave me a hammock on the first floor veranda of his old wooden home next to the mosque. All he asked of me, a non-believer, was not to look over the veranda down on those assembled on Friday to pray. And he told me with regret "*tidak ada white horse*" (there is no white horse whiskey). A well in the backyard supplied drinking and washing water — you sluiced yourself down beside the well at the end of a long day — sanitary conveniences were simple to say the least; but we ate well, chicken, rice, fish, lots of fruit, bananas, pomelos, rambutans in particular, and bread, and one coffee shop sold Anchor beer. The *kathi* (the only Malay I have ever met with four wives) had no scruples in drinking a glass of beer with me, but only alone in my company. He shared his liberal outlook on life with his friend Tunku Abdul Rahman, of the Kedah royal house, who was on his way to a clean sweep of the first ever Federal elections (due in a few months' time on July 27, 1955) and would on August 31, 1957, become Prime Minister of independent Malaya. Merdeka indeed!

For a week we trudged around the padi fields and the edge of the jungle, even venturing by dugout onto the estuary of the Muda and Merboh Rivers. There were some half dozen armed communists on nearby Gunung Jerai, the prominent Kedah mountain that had been for centuries the landfall, of traders crossing the Bay of Bengal, so we were unable to explore it closely. Nevertheless we were successful. Our minor discoveries and subsequent report resulted in a later expedition led by Michael Sullivan that uncovered more tangible evidence uncovered, and then a third group, led by Alistair Lamb, excavated the ruin of a temple on the seaward flank of the mountain by the side of a rushing stream. Lamb led several more groups and discovering more sites identified as of 14th-century origin. The Bujang Valley (Lembah Bujang), with over 30 sites excavated, is now part of Malaysia's national heritage. Reference to our pioneering work is made in the display centre, which was crowded with school children absorbed in it all when we visited it again in 2003.

My own piece of excitement had come one day when we arrived at a small kampong by the Muda River. Shirts stained with sweat, shorts, boots thick with mud, we were invited by the hospitable village headman to come up for a cool drink. We took off our boots and hats and climbed the steps. When scraping the mud from my boots before putting them on again, I noticed that the mud scraper provided at the foot of the steps was of hard cut stone. All Malay buildings in Kedah are of wood and attap. I pointed it out to the Kampong Ketua. Where did it come from? Was it old? It has always been there, I was told. Not so, said another, it had come long ago from the plinth by the river, a phallic symbol, an ancient cut stone they regarded as a *keramat* (a holy shrine). Had we not seen it? He led us to the river bank and I was photographed standing next to it. Later research identified both stones as of Chola (South Indian) origin, possibly 15th century and they are now on display at the Lembah Bujang (Bujang Valley) centre.

Four of the students who were with me that day, pioneers of their kind, have remained my friends. By strange coincidence three of them went on to meritorious careers in the diplomatic service of their respective nations, nations that did not exist when they were undergraduates. Chiang Hai Ding, a top student with a brilliant mind, went on a PhD scholarship to the Australian National University in Canberra, then joined me as a lecturer in the History Department back in Singapore. After I left he was elected to Parliament as a PAP member for Ulu Pandan, then rose through the ranks of the Foreign Service to be ambassador to Germany, to the European Union and finally Egypt, challenging positions that he handled with great success. On retirement in 2002 he took a graduate diploma in Gerontology from Simon Fraser University in Canada and become the executive director of SAGE (Singapore Action Group of Elders) counselling centre.

Joe Conceicao, who had spent several ghastly years during the Japanese era in the notorious Eurasian camp in Johor, was a cheerful companion of mine who on graduation moved into Adult Education, then in 1968 was elected to Parliament as member for Katong. Mr Lee Kuan Yew kept filching our good graduates to serve the nation, and Joe was one of them, going as ambassador to the Soviet Union (twice) and later to Australia (when I caught up with him again).

Aputhnan Nelson had the temerity to give me as a birthday book on his graduation Carola Oman's biography of his namesake, Admiral Nelson. I have it still, along with a clock mounted and inscribed, presented to me when I visited Kuala Lumpur in 2003. He had retired, having been created a Dato, from a fine service in Malaysia's Foreign Service. His good friend, Krishnan Iyer, another of that Kota Kuala Muda group, and who became headmaster of Penang Free School, had shared the gift. In my preface to *The British in Malaya: The First Forty Years 1786–1826*, I thanked them all, well aware that such friendships add a new dimension to the life of any European fortunate to share them.

4 Kuala B'rang

During our time in Singapore the east coast of Malaya remained as it had for centuries, a remote and isolated part of the peninsula. Three states — Pahang, Trengganu and Kelantan — were largely tropical rainforest. Each had one straggling little town by a river mouth — Kuantan, Kuala Trengganu and Kota Bharu — each isolated from the others by other rivers. A single road came over from the thriving west coast, crossing the main mountain range, the backbone of Malaya, near Kuala Lumpur. Few Chinese inhabited the states concerned, and they concentrated in the towns. It was largely a Malay area, and their life, whether fisherman or padi planter, was one of simple poverty and devout worship of Allah.

It was, and is, an attractive part of the world, its beaches in particular, each nestling inside its ubiquitous red cliffs made most attractive by their unspoiled charm. To us at the university 50 years ago it was also interesting in that the earliest signs of Islam in Malaya was a Moslem tombstone near Kuala B'rang (a kampong well from Trengganu's coast) dated the Moslem equivalent of 1303 AD. This was a subject of academic speculation. Malacca on the west coast was for centuries the entrepôt from where Islam spread through Southeast Asia. No one went to the east coast; there was no trade, no port, only the crashing South China Sea. Thousand year old Chinese charts depicted Pulau Tioman off Johor as the island land-fall, but this was to guide Amoy junks to the Malacca Straits. None stopped on the way: or did they? Joseph Needham, the eminent sinologist with an encyclopaedic knowledge of Chinese science, speculated to me that this might have happened: hence the solitary tombstone. Did Islam come to Southeast Asia from China?

It was a good excuse for another archaeological expedition. We drove across to the east coast in an old university mini-bus, leaving Kuala Lumpur in the comparative cool of the early morning. Almost immediately we were labouring up the jungled slopes of the mountains. A scattered settlement of *orang asli*, the indigenous pagans of the interior welcomed us as we crossed the ridge to stop beside the eastward flowing Pahang River. Here, at Temerloh, bored British soldiers who had not seen a terrorist for months, helped us cross the powerful stream. Down to Kuantan on the coast, and then northwards, stopping repeatedly to navigate by cabled barge the many rivers that invited us to pause and cool down. We turned in from the coast at last in Trengganu, heading for the mountains, across padi fields, coconut palms, patches of thick greenery, until in the early evening we reached Kuala B'rang.

Here the road ended. Further movement was possible only on foot or on the river. We stayed in the hostel, a single dormitory, of the local school. It was a very poor kampong, a row of mean wooden shops, really stalls. I could not buy a hat, as only head cloths were worn. No electricity, little water as the well was nearly dry. No fruit, few vegetables. We discovered that not everyone could afford a sarong. The Malay is the most modest of people and to see naked children when we walked through up-river kampongs was distressing.

The Trengganu River was wide but shallow. A swift current and shifting channels made travel a challenge. We went either by poled dugout or on flat little ferries powered by small outboard engines on a number of exploratory expeditions into the *ulu*. We enjoyed the simple, never-changing river life; women washing clothes, boys swimming, buffaloes plodding across cleared *padi* fields. We shouted out greetings to other launches crisscrossing the wide river to avoid the current, all under a blue sky with big white clouds going over to the mountains 20 miles away.

At the scattered huts where the ancient gravestone had been found we met the headman, the Ketua Kampong. He took us on a long walk. The villagers joined in, aroused by this odd event, of 14 Chinese, Malays, Indians and a European. We exchanged good mornings — "Selamat pagi". A dry, hard rice field, where Chinese porcelain peeped through the earth near some fairly recent Moslem tombstones, was the end of our safari. It started to rain, heavily. Wielding heavy hoes, *changkols*, gave us all blisters.

As it turned out our laborious dig here and elsewhere was a failure. We found no further evidence of early Islam. I was so enjoying the experience that I worried little. Each day was a pleasure of exploration. Our cheery Malay cook had shown us a most welcome swimming pool on the B'rang River. Here trees towered up, creepers enabled us to perform acts Tarzan would have envied and the deep water was deliciously cool.

In the evenings, fresh and clean, we would wander down to the kampong's coffee shop after our evening meal of fish and rice, and while the entire village stood outside and watched the *tuan* have his beer, the students would play with their coffee laced with condensed milk, or coke, and courteously talk of their future and my past. The three girls, Chinese and Eurasians, in slacks, no doubt were outrageous in the eyes of the villagers, but of course, as women always do, they kept us civilised.

On our last day in Kuala B'rang we went right into the mountains, a long river trip. Here on a broad sand bank, jungle all around, we were chased by what I thought were crocodiles, ferocious creatures that came charging across the sand bank, but which Sharom Ahmat, a student, assured me were the biggest iguanas he had ever seen. Later, on a long hike, nearly all of us collected leeches on our legs, horrible things. I had met them earlier in the jungle near Sandakan. Renewing the acquaintance was not to my liking. We then turned happily towards the coast.

Kuala Trengganu then was one narrow, curving street around a wide estuary, with a dozen or so big Chinese two-masted trading schooners at anchor. They brought various goods — salt in particular — as well as opium, down from Thailand.

Round this estuary were four or five kampongs, their stilted homes marching into the water. The lovely east coast *prahu* were everywhere, many powered, others with one rectangular sail. These white specks were scattered all over the horizon in the later afternoon, when returning from fishing, but when they came onto the beach the sail always could be seen to be a half dozen or so of bleached Australian flour bags sewn together.

Sharom bought two big fish — *ikan tenggiri* — from one of the fishermen, and then selected the Chinese coffee shop where we had them boiled, together with *bak choy* and other green vegetables for our dinner, sitting out on an open platform over the sea.

Next day we were given a tour of the traditional arts and crafts being encouraged in the kampongs by the state government. This included in several houses batik cloth manufacture, using an ancient technique that originated in Java centuries ago; brass work, most of it committed to mosques; some silver work not as attractive as those I had seen in Brunei; and at another kampong house lovely silk sarongs being made, beautifully woven with silver or gold thread. I was very taken with a royal blue sarong, another of orange with a silver pattern of small flowers (a Buddhist, not Moslem, emblem), but in the end I came away with a piece, black with silver thread, that my wife made into an evening dress.

Finally we met the kris maker, who after showing us some magnificent pieces, all with a *Garuda* at the hilt to demonstrate their Javanese origin, was persuaded to produce a very old one that clearly was of utilitarian, rather than decorative value, a very nasty wavy blade indeed. "Never against an Englishman", we were told. Much laughter. It was a good business, for a kris is an essential part of Malay ceremonial dress.

Further north at Kota Bharu in Kelantan, once part of Siam, a student friend who as a boy had worked unwillingly, so he said for the Japanese kempeitai (army espionage police) took us to a park to see the then only remaining *wayang kulit* or shadow play that was still in existence in Malaya. Again originally from Java, stories from the ancient Hindu epics the Mahabaratta and Ramayana are depicted by artists behind a screen of white cloth. Puppets cut out of leather throw a shadow on the screen, the story teller chants the tale, and the listeners sit entranced. We heard that President Sukarno of Indonesia could watch it for hours. This may be; only the elderly in Kota Bahru were listening, the youngsters were down the road at the Odeon cinema.

The Sultan's son showed us over the Lilliputian fort by the bar at the entrance to the sea. "Oh yes," he said, "the British District Officer was much better than the present one. He visited the *ulu* kampongs regularly, and was not afraid of headquarters, acted on his own initiative. Why even the Perhentians were visited."

I too had visited the Perhentians, remote islands some 50 or more miles off the coast in the South China Sea. As a sub-lieutenant in the MRNVR (Malayan Royal Navy Volunteer Reserve) I had for a number of years spent several hours once a month at its training establishment, a former Japanese minesweeper re-named *Panglima* tied up to the Singapore docks. One weekend exercise had taken us up the east coast, over the clearly discernible wrecks near Tioman Island of *HMS Repulse* and *HMS Prince of Wales*, sunk by the Japanese on December 10, 1941 at the outset of their invasion, and on to these islands.

The few kampongs on Pulau Redang and the Perhentians were inhabited by tough, rough fishermen. Or rather, men who made a living, outside the law, from the sea. We had been warned to be careful, there was no authority, we found them surly and uncooperative. It later became a dumping ground for Vietnamese boat people on whom all sorts of atrocities were committed.

Now I believe the East Coast is all changed. Offshore oil rigs and onshore termini, bridges over all the rivers, new roads from the west, hotels, airfields, a Club Med and tourists galore, with a strong economic pulse replacing the languor of centuries. Remaining, so I understand, is the strong faith of the people, and the mosque courtyard is still the gathering ground of them all.

The unexpected bonus of this Kuala B'rang week was the discovery of Sharom Ahmat. He stood out as the leader of this miscellaneous group of students, asserting authority in a mixed racial group. One of the Chinese Students, who later was to run a successful construction business in the tough competitive environment of Singapore, Khor Buck Chye, was particularly strong. It made no difference. Sharom was in charge.

On return to Singapore I encouraged his progress. A first class Honours Degree (awarded at the same ceremony presided over by Tunku Abdul Rahman in Kuala Lumpur where I gained my doctorate), then a post-graduate scholarship to Brown University in Rhode Island. Here I was able to visit him. He rejoined me on the staff in Singapore, and, after I left, completed his own PhD on Kedah history in London. A career at high educational level followed, including a stint as "academic advisor" in reality Vice-chancellor at the new Brunei University, with his services repeatedly utilised by the Malaysian government and other bodies. Professor Datuk Haji Sharom Ahmat has remained my friend now for over 50 years.

How the Cold Storage Shaped World History

Shortly after our arrival in Singapore in 1953, we discovered one of its unanticipated attractions. This was the year round availability of fresh food, a welcome change from grey post-war London, with its rationing and general shortages. The refrigeration facilities provided by the Singapore Cold Storage Company in particular, which in collaboration with refrigerated ships brought the world's fruits and vegetables, as well as meat, butter and milk to our table, enabled us to live well.

But when the Company was registered here 50 years earlier, on June 8, 1903, it had been a different matter altogether. Singapore then was part of the equatorial Third World, a modern euphemism hiding the horrid facts of life. For what was the position?

Meat was best avoided, or tackled in a curry. Beef came from stringy local buffaloes, with pork more sought after as a traditional Chinese delicacy. Bali, being non-Moslem, had a long standing trade in pigs with Singapore, while the junks of south China also traded, but in both cases the voyage could last a week or more, and with no refrigeration on board deterioration if not disease was hardly avoidable. The *ad hoc* slaughtering of the local cattle was another crime scene.

Indeed it was the lack of acceptable meat in Singapore that provided the initiative for the formation of the Cold Storage. With its eye then largely on a European clientele such as the army contingent as well as civilians based in Singapore, and the regular provisioning demands of the shipping, it saw the probability of a profitable market, while its strong links to the vast cattle stations of Queensland provided it with a guaranteed source of supply.

It was less successful in solving the milk problem. Until the two insulated store-rooms that the Company built at Borneo wharf in Keppel Harbour began operating in 1905, milk was obtained from Bengali vendors who hawked their sickly animals around the streets, milking them when necessary. This thin, bluish white liquid not infrequently flavoured with cow dung was less than popular, and imported condensed or powdered milk was preferred by nearly all in whose diet milk figured.

Rice of course was the staple for the great majority of the population, imported mainly from Siam. Fish was another staple, caught in local waters. Due to the primitive conditions that prevailed, along with the lack of authoritative supervision, this was of a very poor quality indeed, when finally it reached the market. As I was told, before even the fish were landed they lay around in the small *prahu* of the Malay fisherman sometimes for days, in a warm mixture of bilge water, blood and slime at the bottom of the boat. This produced the dull looking and sour smelling fish already in the early stages of decomposition that were offered for sale.

Hardly any fruit other than a poor supply of tropical bananas and such like, augmented by oranges from South China were available. Lemons, for some unexplained reason, never grew east of Suez, but lime, from Java, was a delightful substitute, parti-cularly when mixed with gin. Potatoes also came across from Java. The few market gardeners who supplied local beans and other poor quality vegetables were helped considerably in growing their produce from the hard red earth of the island by the age old practice of utilising human manure.

All in all, the food then available made Singapore a less than desirable location, nor did the general environment help. No municipal sewerage system or a night soil disposal organisation was introduced until 1914. I can recall talking about these early days with a group of prominent business men including Lee Kong Chian, the university benefactor. He came down to Singapore aged seven in 1902, the son of a poor tailor. He could vividly remember Chinese "coolies" as they were then called (a disparaging long standing term now thankfully forgotten) jogging down somnolent Orchard Road and the town's more crowded main streets, balancing on their shoulder the swaying long pole with a bucket of night soil at either end, apprehensive rickshaws and other pedestrians avoiding them with difficulty. If the night soil was not sold, into the river it was dumped, so I was told.

Electricity was not installed until 1906, and even then it was confined to a few private consumers, mainly Import and Export Agencies with offices along Collyer Quay, where an electric tram service had begun the previous year. The main illuminator however was kerosene, supplied by a small Dutch firm that had just started in Sumatra, named Shell.

There were no cars on the island but by 1903 a privately constructed railway was operating from the docks to a stop where Newton Circus is today (crossing Orchard Road by a bridge) and then out to Bukit Timah village and through the jungle and the scattered plantations to Kranji. However this was very much the back door. A few tracks led out of the town, one to Tanglin where lived the *tuans*, and one or two others; but they were little used except by the Chinese working in the market gardens. Tigers that swam across to the island from Johor regarded the rainforest, and the wild pigs roaming in it, as theirs — one was found asleep under the billiard table of the Tanglin Club, so goes the story — and most of Singapore's attention, as with the newly established Cold Storage, was on the crowded, bustling river, harbour and waterfront.

Here on March 24, 1905 the first ever cargo of frozen goods to Singapore, 370 tons of beef, mutton, lamb and fresh butter, arrived from Brisbane on the S.S. Guthrie. Hailed with delight, within days much of it was virtually inedible, rotten, impregnated with tar that had melted on the roof of its newly installed refrigerated godown. And with this we step up onto the world stage.

Japan and Russia were at war. After a year of conflict it was going very badly for the Russians. Contemptuous of this Asian midget, ill informed about its naval and military capability, Imperial Russia's incompetent leaders had committed its armies to land actions such as Liaoyang in Manchuria, then Mukden, the biggest battles Man had ever fought, which left it staggering. What followed is a well-known story, how in late 1904 Admiral Zinovy Petrovich Rozhdestvensky, commander of the Imperial Russian Baltic Fleet (renamed the Second Pacific Squadron) was ordered by the Czar to take it to Vladivostok in Siberia, there to redeem Russian prestige and to teach the Japanese a lesson they would never forget.

After an agonising journey begun in October which had taken it down the Baltic, followed by the North Sea and South Atlantic, around the Cape of Good Hope then a laborious haul across the Indian Ocean, mishaps, delays and blunders all the way, on April 8 the fleet staggered past Raffles Light, off Singapore. Note the date: just a few weeks after S.S. Guthrie began unloading its refrigerated cargo, which by then had turned rancid or rotten.

Our local paper *The Straits Times* described the scene as thousands of people that day crowded the *padang* shore to watch the long line of ships, 47 of them, steaming slowly towards Horsborough Light seven miles out to sea, with black smoke belching from their funnels and thick seaweed growth streaming along every waterline. Rebuffed by neutral countries throughout its six month journey, the fleet was in dire straits.

The Russian consul in Singapore was trying desperately to help. He contacted H.W. Stevens, the Cold Storage manager. He could not supply coal but was prepared quietly to disregard the neutrality of Great Britain and sell a recently arrived cargo of meat. Not for the first time, and certainly not the last, Singapore government regulations were bypassed by a pragmatic businessman.

By lunch the consul sped out to the passing fleet. He carried instructions from St. Petersburg for it to rendezvous in Camranh Bay, in French Indo-China, to wait there for other ships coming from Russia. And there he would deliver not merely the Cold Storage cargo, but also a Chinese cook for the Admiral, a bonus gift from Stevens. (He never arrived.)

In their *The Tide at Sunrise: A History of the Russo-Japanese War 1904-1905*, Denis and Peggy Warner describe in detail the fleet wide sickness, diarrhoea, and near mutiny that resulted once the Singapore provisions were taken on board. Morale already low sank even further.

The fleet staggered on. To its north the Japanese were ready and waiting. Highly trained and disciplined, eager for action, manning modern ships and brilliantly led by Admiral Heihachiro Togo, they intercepted the Russians in the Straits of Tsushima off southern Japan. Here on May 27-28 was fought the most dramatic and decisive sea battle for a hundred years. With the exception of two small Russian vessels that fled to Manila, the entire battle fleet of 35 ships was sunk, captured or interned.

Tsushima was a naval victory of immense political significance. Riots in Russia shook the empire and ushered in ten years of unrest leading to revolution. In Asia following an early peace came the extension of Japanese power over Korea, then unchallenged into Manchuria, while the incredible news that an Asian country had defeated an Imperialist European power raised expectation and renewed hopes all over Asia for independence. It was seen from India to Indonesia as the beginning of the slow swing back of history's pendulum, which since the time of Vasco da Gama had established European dominance over the continent.

Even 50 years after the event, when I demonstrated to my Singapore students on my Bukit Timah blackboard how Togo's masterly manoeuvres, particularly his "crossing of the T" when by superior speed he daringly turned his battle columns across the head of the long line of Russian ships, so that he could pour overwhelmingly broadsides into them, and how the victor of Pearl Harbour, Yamamoto, also was there, the response was electric.

Without doubt, the battle of Tsushima was one of the most significant events in modern Asian history. The rotten beef from Australia and the role in this played by the Singapore Cold Storage deserves a mention.

Staff, Department of History, University of Singapore, Oct. 1966. Front row, from left: Sharom Ahmat, Jenny Choong, Mary Rayner, Ken Tregonning, Eunice Thio, Irene Ee, Wong Lin Ken; Back row, from left: Yeoh Kim Wah, Edwin Lee, R. Suntharalingam, Chiang Hai Ding, Yong Ching Fatt, Png Poh Seng, Mat (Mohd. Ibrahim bin Baba).

Interview with President Macapagal at the President's Palace, Manila, Feb. 1963. Left to right: Minister of Foreign Affairs Emmanuel Pelaez, President Macapagal, Domingo A. Abella, Ken Tregonning.

Farewell dinner for K.G. Tregonning, 1966. The person seated in the centre is George E. Bogaars, later head of Singapore's independent civil service and Permanent Secretary for the Ministry of Defence.

Sungei Muda, Kedah, 1954.

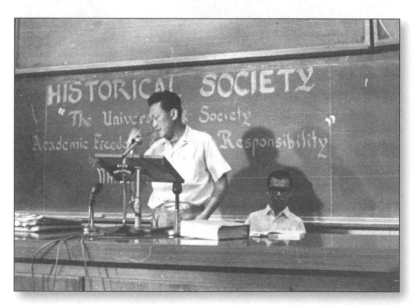

The Hon. Lee Kuan Yew speaks to the University of Singapore Historical Society, 1966. Seated: Tan Chin Tiong, President of the Historical Society of the University of Singapore.

History students and staff, University of Malaya, 1953.

A snapshot of my multi-racial old friends using my new camera.

Two readers of *Fajar* eye one another suspiciously at the Royal Singapore Yacht Club, 1954.

"Kajang" leaving Jesselton, North Borneo, 1953.

The author with Mr. R. Gillett, the supervisor of the workshops of the North Borneo Government Railways at the Jesselton Railway, North Borneo, 1959.

Saturday afternoon tea with Jenni and Judy at the Royal Singapore Yacht Club.

Sailing at Changi Yacht Club.

6 Borneo

As usual, that morning there was hardly a breath of breeze. We passed a gaily painted *jong kong*, almost becalmed, her sails slack. Only the bow wave of our sturdy government launch broke the calm. We had left behind "pirate point" as the northernmost tip of Borneo had been called for centuries. Ahead was Balambangan Island. Although a brave little Union Jack fluttered at our stern, we were in troubled waters. Lawless islands were to our east and north. The Sulu Sea was not for the timid. The crew chief, the *serang*, handed his rifle to the Dato. But we need not have feared.

We anchored, then in our dinghy ran up onto the beach. Casuarina pines lined the bay. Behind were some hillocks covered in rather scruffy jungle. On one side was a small clearing with several wood and attap huts on stilts. From them came a small group of people. We had understood that this rarely visited island was uninhabited, with a kampong or two on the larger Banggi Island nearby. But here were half a dozen Banggi Dusuns clad only in loincloths called *chawats*. They glanced at me in surprise as a rare European, in awe at my companion, Mustapha bin Dato Harun.

I had come to this island in order to see where the British East India Company had in 1773 established its first trading post in Southeast Asia. Penang in 1786, then Singapore in 1819 were subsequent successes, lighting the way to Hong Kong in 1848, but this first venture led nowhere. It was attacked by Suluks on March 5, 1775, the settlement stockade stormed and torched, the godown looted, the sepoys killed or enslaved. John Herbert, the Factor in charge of the post, and a few others were fortunate to flee. The Company never returned.

I became aware of this disaster when at Oxford. As a lead-in to my research on the British North Borneo Chartered Company, I had set myself, as a necessary preliminary, the pleasure of reading every book published in England on Borneo. The Bodleian, by Act of Parliament, is entitled to receive a copy of each and every book published in the UK, so sitting comfortably in Duke Humfrey's Library for several months, as the snow fell softly on gentle hills and ancient colleges all around, this I did.

One such book which gave an eye-witness account of the 1775 episode was T. Forrest's, *A Voyage To New Guinea from Balambangan*, published in 1780. Fetched for me from its repository far away along one of the Bodleian tunnels that run under Oxford, it had taken two days for it to be retrieved. When placed before me I discovered that its leaves were uncut. I was the first person in nearly 200 years to read it. Whenever after that I attempted to write a book I had to hope this horrible fate would never happen to me. So far I think I have been successful. But let the tunnels of the Bodleian be a warning to all prospective authors.

I collected several 18th-century potshards that day on Balambangan, broken pieces of China pottery, had lunch with Mustapha and the *serang* — bananas and bread for me — and was deterred from swimming in the limpid blue waters, hot though it was at noon, by talk of Portuguese men-of-war, thick welts on the *serang*'s leg proving his point. We returned to Kudat that afternoon. The British government had invited me in 1957 to write a book on North Borneo (for which Winston Churchill later was to provide a preface) and here I was on a Singapore university vacation beginning a three-month tour.

Next afternoon the Kudat district officer — or to give him the capitals to which he was due, The District Officer, (for he

was the most important person in that part of the Colony) —
had a select gathering of local notables for me. We stood on his
lawn overlooking the immense Marudu Bay and I talked again to
the dato, his assistant. He was not merely the Assistant District
Officer however. As *Orang Kaya Kaya*, Dato Mustapha bin Dato
Harun was the most powerful chief in North Borneo. He was
a member of the newly-established legislative and the rarefied
Executive Council, but his easy exercise of authority had little to
do with colonial patronage.

I was to meet him several more times during my wanderings
and in subsequent visits to the Colony. One in particular I recall
vividly. I was travelling on *Marudu*, one of the Straits Steamships
that in those days maintained a weekly service from Singapore
to Sandakan, and occasionally on to Tawau. We had just left the
Malawali channel that leads around the northeast coast of Borneo
from Kudat to Sandakan where we were to dock next morning.
You have to dodge innumerable minute islands, cays and reefs
that line your path. It was pouring with rain, early evening.

Suddenly our engine stopped. I heard shouting. I raced out
on deck, clad only in a sarong. An arc light shone down on a
wildly tossing government launch. A Bajau seaman beside me
saw him riding out the storm, in his element, said with pride
"Dato Mustapha". He swung himself up and greeted me as he
came on board, not as the slim shy figure at the government
garden party, neat in white shirt and slacks who talked to me of
his famous father, Dato Harun, not as a British-appointed ADO,
but as a barefoot Suluk chief, a dark dagger of a man, his power
exercised far beyond the European-made boundaries of Borneo.

Indeed this was one fundamental fact relating to Southeast
Asia that I first glimpsed through my contact with this leader. As
I was later to learn, most of the independent countries that were
then emerging from under the colonial blanket had boundaries
given them by the earlier European-based history of the region.
They bore little resemblance to their own pre-colonial past, indeed
even assuming that as a state they had such a past.

Thailand's boundaries of 1956 were not those of earlier Siam but those imposed by the rivalry of French and British imperialists. The boundaries of the Burma of 1957 bore little resemblance to those of the earlier kingdom of Ava. Indonesia was another, artificial conglomeration put together by the Dutch, and bearing little resemblance to the ancient Javanese Madjapahit, while the Moslem area of the southern Philippines, at which Mustapha and I were looking, represented an inheritance of failed Spanish imperialism that Catholic Manila never absorbed. Brunei's boundaries are perhaps the most bizarre of the lot, thanks to Charles Brooke. We cannot anticipate that these fictitious boundaries ever will be rectified but they help explain the continuing uncertainties and disturbances of the ethnic minorities inside their borders, ruled as they are by masters often alien to their faith and indifferent to their future.

Mustapha was not to remain a minor cog in the colonial machine for long. Activated by the call of the newly independent Malaya, the creation of Malaysia intended to include the colony of Singapore and the two British Borneo colonies of Sarawak and North Borneo, and political parties — largely racially based — emerged. By 1963, when North Borneo became part of this new Southeast Asian state, Mustapha, by now a Tun, was the political leader of all the Moslem groups in the territory. He became Head of State of Sabah. I was to meet in Asia many more famous than he, but none do I hold higher in my regard, for to use Primo Levi's phrase "here was a man!"

North Borneo was renamed Sabah by its chief minister Donald Stephens shortly after it joined Malaysia in 1963. I had met Stephens ten years before, in 1953, when on my first extended visit to North Borneo I stepped ashore at Labuan Island. It had been the scene a few years earlier of some fierce fighting between Australian and Japanese troops. Signs of that conflict were still visible. A local market or *tamu* was operating at the land end of an army built jetty where our ship *Kajang* had made fast. Nearby the skeleton of a stranded landing craft was embedded in the mangrove. A supercilious young colonial officer checked my credentials. They included a letter from Sir Neil Malcolm, the chairman of the British North Borneo (chartered) Company — which had administered the territory 1881–1941 — to the governor, Sir Roland Turnbull. He read it with new respect and approved my entry to the Colony. Then in subsequent conversation he introduced me to Donald Stephens, a stocky young Eurasian who had detached himself from a chattering group of Brunei Malays, Bajaus, Chinese and others. I had read of the participation of his father Jules Stephens in the Albert Kwok revolt in 1943 and his execution by the Japanese. I was delighted to meet him. I was 30, he much the same age. We hit it off immediately, helped perhaps by our shared Australian heritage.

For centuries the indigenous inhabitants of North Borneo were known as Dusuns. The various Moslem groups on the coast, be they Brunei Malays, Suluks, Bajau or whatever, regarded them as country yokels, good for growing *padi* but not much else. Once pagan, Christian missionaries from the 19th century onwards had been converted and educated. There arose among them resentment at their derogatory label and their inferior status. A desire grew to establish more clearly a position of equality with other Borneo-based races. In this they were led by Donald Stephens.

He came from Penampang, a Dusun Kampong behind Jesselton (as the capital was then called). Its Christian inhabitants were known as Kadazans, and Stephens seized on this name as a replacement of the derogatory "Dusun". When I met him he had established a newspaper, little more than a broadsheet. I bought a copy at the *tamu*, the *British North Borneo News* and *Sabah Times*. It was printed in English and Kadazan. As the only paper in the Colony, it was read by virtually all the literate population. Its influence, so Roland Turnbull told me, was significant; and beneficial.

Stephens helped make my 1953 visit most rewarding, even more so when I returned (after my book on the Chartered Company had been published) in 1957. I recall in particular one rather relaxed evening at Penampang when I joined him and other young Kadazans in *samazau* dancing, with a row of barefoot Kadazan beauties in black and gold advancing and retreating, the crescendo of the bamboo pipes rising and falling as they never but not quite yielded to the circling arms of the men they faced.

On a more serious note I claim some credit for altering the map of Asia, for when independence inside Malaysia became a reality, I wrote to suggest Jesselton as a name was a European name, as irrelevant as the state's title of North Borneo. Stephens already was using Sabah in his newspaper as the alternative. I urged him to make it official. This he did, while my suggestion that Jesselton (named after Sir Charles Jessel, a Vice President of the Chartered Company who had never been there) be named "Singga Mata" ("where the eye loves to dwell") was changed by him to the more effective Kota Kinabalu — the fort of Mt. Kinabalu, Sabah's most distinctive feature.

I take pride too in having suggested that the slopes of that mountain that had looked down on the unspeakable atrocities committed by the Japanese as thousands of Australian prisoners died in their infamous Sandakan camps or on the way to Ranau in 1944–45, should become a national memorial park. In 1953, to reach Ranau, I had to fly, for neither leading to or in Ranau itself, then a small kampong high in the jungle interior where the final barbaric acts were performed, were there any roads. Today it is the centre of a national park where scores of Japanese tourists step from their coaches to admire the roses growing there, in a memorial to those their kinfolk killed.

Donald Stephens, chief minister of Sabah, was killed with many of his cabinet, in July 1976 in a mysterious crash as his plane was coming in to land at Kota Kinabalu. His role, in merging all Kadazan groups into a dynamic whole, and then cooperating with Tun Mustapha's Moslem parties, had given Sabah nearly two decades of stability and growth. I remember both these historic figures as friends, Sabah itself, this "land below the wind" with nostalgic affection.

7 The Padang

Heavy rain had closed our hatches for several hours. We were still at anchor when our scheduled sailing time came. Our winches whined and clattered. Chinese labourers shouted to their companions down below shouting back, as our derricks hauled up cargo from the *twakows* (barges) hard against us. I sat on deck in a rattan arm chair, watching this frantic yet disciplined effort. A warm evening fell. The lights of Singapore and those on other ships anchored nearby, their cables taut against the pulling tide, shone on the turgid water. Beyond them was the land. We were directly opposite the graceful old cathedral, built by convicts a hundred years earlier (1856–62) and the even older park, the village green of Singapore, the padang.

It had been the custom in particular for the well-to-do of all races of 19th-century Singapore to circle the *padang* in their carriages in the comparative cool of the late afternoon. As I sat back with a cold beer for company I was reminded of the tale of the young civil servant who imported an elegant carriage and a pair of prancing ponies from Hong Kong. His wife, as she bowed to the others, even to the wife of the governor, was sure that she sat in the smartest carriage of them all. Next morning he was summoned before His Excellency. "You'll have to get rid of that carriage, m'boy," he was told. "But why sir?" he asked, nervous but bristling, with a sense of petticoat interference. "Those Chinese characters on the door; know what they mean?" "No sir. I thought they were merely attractive symbols for long life and good luck."

"Nothing of the sort. They say 'my name is Mai Lun, and my price is ten dollars.'"

Mai Lun has long gone, but the *padang* has remained, the core of Singapore. No other Chinese city has this green heart. It is the legacy of Stamford Raffles, when in 1819 he laid out the initial plans for this new settlement. The *padang* has survived the centuries unscathed, witness not merely to the passing peccadilloes and pleasures of its people, but a participant as well in the humiliation, excitement and pride of the island's history.

In 1942, to go no further back in that history, all those Europeans on the island who had not fled, men, women and children, joined all the defeated British-led troops assembled there on February 17, before they began the long march to Salarang or Changi. July 5, 1943 had it playing host again to a packed concourse of troops, this time the Indian National Army volunteers and opportunists who marched past its commander, Chandra Bose, under the watchful eye of the Japanese Premier, Tojo. A wildly cheering crowd occupying every conceivable vantage place packed the padang on September 12, 1945, when Lord Louis Mountbatten took the salute at the Victory Parade, having earlier accepted there the surrender of the Japanese forces. And then later the padang came to be used for stirring National Day parades or on other significant occasions.

One such occasion in which we participated was in early 1954. Tan Lark Sye, leader of the Hokkien community and multi-millionaire President of the Chinese Chamber of Commerce, had 1,000 guests to a banquet there. Following a congratulatory telegram to Mao Tse Tung on the communist accession to power in China, he had called for the establishment in Singapore of a Chinese-language university. This dinner was to report progress, as its building in Jurong began to overshadow the modest English-language university at Bukit Timah. The concept had aroused great excitement among the mass of Chinese proud of the success of their homeland. The colonial government (and the English-speaking element of the community) were appalled. The dinner, where thousands of spectators crowded against rope barriers, gave a most disturbing implication of a divided country.

By 1954 hundreds of Chinese students were leaving for China each month, while the thousands who remained, attending the Chinese-language Middle Schools into their early 20s, were dominated by the fanatical activists already indoctrinated by their anti-colonial pro-communist teachers. Singapore was a classic example of a state with two incompatible education systems. Its collapse could be anticipated. The skilful exit of the colonial power and the political genius of Lee Kuan Yew in merging these two streams removed that possibility; but it was a close run thing, and both were in the future when we listened to Tan Lark Sye. It was with foreboding that we left the *padang* that night. Was Singapore to become an Asian Cuba?

However we stayed, optimistically working for a non-communist independent nation, and here I am years later sipping my beer and watching as our anchor is cranked up. We sailed at midnight. Carefully we threaded our way out to an uncluttered South China Sea. In those days out from the *padang* a detached breakwater built in 1911–14 gave shelter to the little trading ships of Singapore. The not so small, such as *Keningau* on which I was travelling, were anchored further out. Always, at any time of the day or night, there would rarely be less than 50 such vessels. Often many more. A crowded anchorage, then and now. Perhaps it is not too much to say that here, along with the padang, is the heart of Singapore.

Many of those anchored near us that night had come south after China had collapsed to the communists in 1949. A heterogeneous collection of river and coastal craft was forced then to find another home. Some came here, to compete with the local craft trading with the nearby Indonesian islands. The disturbed conditions in these waters suited them. In 1963 however, when Sukarno's "confrontation" came, they were hit hard. All trade from Singapore with Sumatra, the nearby Rhio Archipelago, Kalimantan, Java and elsewhere was stopped. Officially that is; there were still a few ways of slipping through.

Obscured now by high rise hotels and other complexes, in those days the nearest of these nearby islands were visible from the *padang*. The shop keepers and traders there had had credit arrangements with their Singapore counterparts for generations. Neither side was anxious to see this ended. The good currency of Singapore and the plentiful stocks of useful commodities were assets lacking in Indonesia. Javanese control was far away. Various devices were resorted to. Vessels would leave Singapore with one set of papers. They would arrive in an Indonesian port with a totally different set. These would show they came not from Singapore but from some other port. Sihanoukville in Cambodia became a useful entrepot. Ill paid army and custom officers in charge of outlying islands found it convenient and profitable to quietly acquiesce in this. Corruption has long been a way of life in Southeast Asia. It flourished under these conditions. So by one way or another Singapore-Indonesian trade was maintained.

Some ships however were forced to seek other routes. One of these was to Sarawak. By 1964 nine small Chinese-operated lines were competing where only two had sailed before. They were eager for any trade at all. They offered exceptionally low freight rates, as they made no provision for insurance, depreciation, maintenance or replacement. Wages were low for the minimum crew. It was a fierce fight. Many suffered.

Amongst others, the position of the old established Sarawak Steamship Company became precarious. It had a history going back to the days of the White Rajah in the mid-19th century. This little helped. It was a responsible firm which kept its ships in good condition. It could not reduce its rates to those offered by this jackel pack. It lost considerably. However, a number of factors began to work in its favour. A damaged cargo on the competing lines would not be insured. It could be a complete loss. The shipper could expect no compensation. Few vessels sailed on regular schedules. Shippers could not plan for delivery. One turned over in Kuching River, due to faulty loading. Other hazards became apparent. These persuaded some shippers to return to Sarawak

Steam, which insured its cargoes, met all claims, travelled on schedule and never turned over.

During this time it had been helped by its close ties with another responsible shipping firm, Straits Steamship which operated a service to Kuching and on to Sabah. It had run this service since 1915, when it replaced a German line. It had an even earlier association with the river ports of the Malay Peninsula. Its small vessels, including two paddle steamers, had traded with them from Singapore since 1890. Since that time the history of the Company was essentially the history of its home port. It was my good luck to be invited by it to write that history. This resulted in *Home Port Singapore: A History of Straits Steamship Company, 1890–1965*, published by Oxford University Press (1967). A trip to Borneo had been part of the bargain, so here I was with my cold beer waiting to sail.

With all cargo loaded we left our anchorage in the early evening. *Keningau* was formerly a Dutch vessel, of 4,856 tons, bought from the KPM when Sukarno had forced the company out of Indonesia, which was a political move of disastrous economic consequences for an empire of islands joined only by the sea. Beside my bunk was a protuberance from the cabin wall, a device used for polishing Mijnheer's monocle. The Achenese crew kept the ship spotlessly clean, a legacy of their Dutch training.

All Sunday we ploughed across the South China Sea. I was taken below to be shown by the *chinchew* how a consignment of eggs, shipped to Kuching at a minimum freightage rate, had become chickens by arrival in Sarawak, to be unloaded before a higher rate was applied to them. Emerging on deck the post-war *Vyner Brooke* passed us, heading back to Singapore. She dipped her ensign in salute. We reciprocated. Her namesake fleeing from Singapore had been sunk by the Japanese in 1942, during the Pacific war. The passengers, including a number of Australian nurses, were subsequently massacred. Later I was to meet the solitary survivor, Sister Bullwinkle, and hear her horrible story.

At dawn next morning we reached the Borneo coast. I was on deck again as we entered the Sarawak River for Kuching with the mangrove nearly brushing our bows, the jungle stretching away, Mount Santubong towering close by, Dyaks in dugouts, Ibans in kolehs, and Tom Harrisson along with Bujang Mohamed, one of my early graduates waiting to meet me. Then on to Kuala Belait up the coast; where I hoped for confirmation from the Shell executives working the oil field of the rumour in Singapore that seismic surveys way offshore in the Spratly Islands gave signs of an immense oil field. No one lived there, no country claimed this area of reefs and islets, and it was a hazard all shipping whether sail or steam had avoided; so what if it contained an underwater Saudi Arabia? Whose would it be?

Brunei was to be my next port of call. Here were several Brunei friends and I would see Kampong Ayer, unchanged for centuries, the description of the Portuguese Pigafetta in 1521 still valid. Jesselton next, where an Anglo-Indian ran a quaint little railway whose blundering and incompetent construction in the late 19th century I had followed with horror through official documents, that was to take me into Borneo's interior.

Sandakan also was on my agenda, where hopefully I would visit again the guano-filled Gomantong caves after a day of trudging through mangrove and jungle. Here I was to enquire whether anyone remembered Tuan Keith, the pre-war Superintendent of Forestry, whose wife, Agnes, had written the classics *Below The Wind* and *Three Came Home*. (And when indeed I got there, "Yes" was the warm answer from many of the villagers.) All a long way from Singapore and its *padang*.

8 Tea Cups and Tokyo

Not long after returning to Singapore on *Keningau*, her chief engineer, Alan Ferguson, invited me home to meet his wife Violet. They lived in one of the Straits Steamship Flats in Sommerville Estate, and she was to fill in the details, so I understood, of their extraordinary wartime experience. Alan, a quietly spoken slightly deaf 50-year-old Ulsterman, was but one of several score Company employees, from chairman to *chinchews* who I interviewed for *Home Port Singapore*, covering the length and breadth of England and Scotland one bitterly cold winter (as well as in Singapore and adjacent areas) in order to do so. With Alan I maintained a friendly acquaintance, nurtured by our Borneo voyage, until his death in 1968.

In May 1940, so he told me on that voyage, he and his wife were in France, she recovering from an appendectomy operation and a miscarriage. They were caught unawares by the German invasion but managed narrowly to escape, sailing for England from Bordeaux in a ferry packed with refugees, almost the last vessel to leave the port. Heaving a sigh of relief they sailed from Liverpool on September 24, happy to be returning to a peaceful East.

They did enjoy a long and peaceful journey, but it came to an abrupt end early on the morning of November 11. Their ship, the Blue Funnel *Automedon* had crossed the Indian Ocean and was due at Penang the next day. She never made it, being intercepted by the German merchant raider *Atlantis*. Summoned to stop, *Automedon* sent out a distress call. This sealed her fate. Struck by several salvos fired from the raider, within a few minutes her radio was destroyed along with most of her superstructure, her steering smashed, most of her officers and crew killed or wounded. She lay a floating wreck motionless in the water.

It had been another swift and successful attack, led by Captain Bernard Rogge. He and his Adjutant, Ulrich Mohr, were remarkably humane officers, and repeatedly in their years at sea in *Atlantis* helped survivors in many ways. In this instance Rogge told the surviving passengers who had been transferred to *Atlantis* that they were going to Germany, a cold country, and he hoped they would have some warm clothes. Frantically Mrs Ferguson pleaded that her trunk, down in the hold, be brought up and passed over.

Rogge signalled across to Mohr who was preparing to sink *Automedon* and anxious to depart the scene. He obeyed orders however and went below with a search party. It stumbled on the strong room. Here was all "unwanted on voyage" luggage, including not one but two trunks of Mrs Ferguson. One contained clothes, the other some crockery, including a tea set. She wanted only the clothes but Rogge insisted and both trunks were transferred to *Atlantis*, along with other material found there, including some mail bags.

Automedon then was sunk and *Atlantis* headed southwest across the Indian Ocean. The group of survivors, some thirty of them, spent four weeks on her before being transferred to a captured Norwegian ship *Storstadt*. It held nearly 500 prisoners from eight other ships sunk by *Atlantis*, with Mrs Ferguson, so she told me, the only woman. Rounding South Africa far to the south of Cape Town, keeping well clear of shipping routes, they sailed up the Atlantic unobserved, finally in March 1941 to slip into Bordeaux.

Here they were separated. Alan with the trunk of crockery went to a camp in northern Germany near Hamburg where captured merchant seamen were held. Violet went to a woman's internment camp near Ravensburg in the south. Finding that the camp was desperately short of tableware she wrote to Alan. The trunk was sent to her; but when the International Red Cross came to the rescue the crockery was repacked and sent back north.

In March 1943 she was repatriated to England and later Alan too, a frail man, in February 1945. With the war over they returned to Singapore. On the eve of their departure they were informed by the British military authorities that they had received Violet's luggage from Germany. It had been kept in a large warehouse outside Hamburg. Not a single item had been lost or broken. It followed them back to Singapore and when Violet poured tea for me at her home it was served from that very tea set.

But the story continues. The Fergusons never knew (nor did I until years later), but among the bags of mail hurriedly brought back onto *Atlantis* from *Automedon* Mohr had found a wealth of confidential British despatches to the British Commander in Chief. They included Admiralty instructions to the Far East naval headquarters, course directions, secret log books, information concerning minefields in Asian waters, new code tables for the fleet, plans and charts showing swept areas, and many more documents including a War Cabinet report with a Confidential Annex giving a summary on the defence of the Far East.

The jackpot that delighted the incredulous two as they pored over them was contained in a narrow green mail bag, weighted for sinking and marked "Classified Destroy in an Emergency". When opened it held a submission by the British Joint Chiefs of Staff Committee on the situation in the Far East, dated July 31, 1940, and the deliberations on it by the War Cabinet on August 8. The former contained precise and detailed information on RN and RAF strength and positions throughout the area, while the latter — with the unmistakeable imprimatur of the Prime Minister Winston Churchill — gave the Cabinets' response to the basic question of how to respond to any possible aggression by the Japanese in Southeast Asia.

Its main decision as expressed in paragraphs 11–12, was "we must avoid an open clash with Japan. A general settlement, including economic concessions to Japan, should be concluded

as soon as possible. Our general policy must be to play for time."
It added "we are faced with the problem of defending our interests
in the Far East without an adequate fleet". (Paragraph 15)

A few days later Captain Rogge rendezvoused with *Ole Jacob*,
a captured Norwegian freighter and transferred all these papers to
her. She arrived in Kobe in early December, flouting the neutrality
of Japan. All the Norwegian and Swedish crew members were
released, to return home via the Trans Siberian Railway. The cache
of documents was sent to Tokyo, to the German Naval Attache,
Admiral Wenneker. Astonished at their depth of information and
convinced of their profound significance, he had copies made of
them all.

Eiki Seki, a former member of Japan's post-war Foreign Service,
in his detailed piece of research *Mrs Ferguson's Tea Set, Japan
and the Second World War* (2007) relates how Wenneker passed
these over to Admiral Nobutake Kondo, the deputy chief of the
Japanese Naval General Staff and how then all Japanese naval
apprehensions that a surge south into Indo-China would provoke
British retaliation were dispelled. Up to this time Japanese army
aggressiveness had been resisted by the navy. But British weakness so revealed, and its policy of avoiding a clash as it had no
fleet, nor any desire to fight, came as a revelation. Seiji quotes
Foreign Minister Matsuoka on December 27 "Britain was too weak
to go to war."

With the Japanese navy convinced by these documents that
its way into Southeast Asia was clear its opposition to a military
expansion became muted. Admiral Isoroku Yamamoto, planning
his attack on Pearl Harbour, went ahead without worrying about
any British response on his rear. The Imperial Navy swung behind
the government. The documents obtained from *Automedon* when
Mohr was searching for Mrs Ferguson's trunk and given to the
Japanese, said Seiki, were a gift of doom.

9 Meeting the Mighty

The arrival from "home" of one of Britain's majestic post-war ocean liners was still a major event in our early Singapore years. Shop fronts in High Street or North Bridge Road would display a metal union jack over the 5 foot way, or a sign "Ship Arrived", telling the initiated (as it must have done for 50 years or more) that a ship from England had berthed and there were goods from it for sale.

This did not prevail for long. Soon enough ripples of Japan's astonishing resurgence reached Singapore. Its goods, synthetic cloths and garments, porcelain, cutlery, crockery, electronics, the transistor radio, cameras and their cars pushed the union jack aside. The freighters still came, to crowd the wharves and anchorage, but they too, were increasingly non-British in origin, replaced by the powerful post-war vessels of Japan, while the passenger liner became a thing of the past.

But before this happened, I recall early in our time we had been browsing in town, firstly in Change Alley off Clifford Pier, which then rivalled Simon Artz of Port Said where for decades ignorant travellers to the Orient purchased junk — but where astute haggling could still satisfy both parties concerned — and then in Robinsons of Raffles Place, then a large newly air conditioned European-style store of several floors. All round Raffles Place small metallic union jacks were on display. One was outside G.C. de Silva's, the jewellers. Here I made a fatal mistake.

Confident that I had no money and never intending to buy it anyway, I ventured to enquire the price of what was clearly a high quality watch which my wife was admiring. It was very expensive, so I thanked young Mr de Silva telling him we were just window shopping and in fact had no money. "Oh that's all right *tuan*, you take it now for your *mem*, you pay me next week." I was taken aback. "How do you know I'll be here next week?" I asked. "I could be a passenger on that P&O liner in port." His trust I thought unbelievable. "No *tuan*, you not a traveller, you live here. Your *mem* like the watch, you take it, pay next week." Obviously I could not lose face, so we left with an expensive Rolex watch on her wrist.

Another early shopping experience involved Malcolm Mac-Donald, the British High Commissioner. He had been helping refugees from the People's Republic of China by authenticating, with a personal note on official vice regal note paper, the valuables they were forced to sell to start again. We would see in High Street shop windows the occasional Tang dynasty horse, or Ming vase, with this note signed by the High Commissioner propped beside it. It gave a guarantee accepted without question.

Once we saw a Sung dynasty bowl, an exquisite piece of light blue porcelain, in Helen Ling's quality shop in Tanglin. Chinese porcelain perhaps had reached its pinnacle of beauty and quality with this dynasty (960–1279 CE). I was looking at a very valuable and very expensive piece of fragile Kiangsi pottery, its survival under such circumstances amazing. I could not but reflect it had been crafted at a time when in England illiterate Norman barons were still close to a life-style of savage brutality, their culture far below that of China.

Of course I could not afford this Sung survival, but memory of it went into my account of the dynasty when in my *World History to 1511 for Malayans* I stressed the role of Asia long neglected in all previous accounts of world history. The book, together with its Bahasa Malaysia translation, was inflicted on secondary school students throughout Malaya and Singapore for a quarter of a century. So Malcolm MacDonald has a lot to answer for.

To my regret we never met, and the role he played in those early momentous years has never been fully explored. As the last pro-consul of Britain's Far East Empire, his subtle, behind the scenes and sympathetic role awaits the historian. Hopefully such a scholar would capture the affection MacDonald shared with peoples of all walks of life, not merely the poor refugees from China.

The British (and Dutch) passenger liners on a regular schedule were replaced during this period — once the jet engine was developed — by aircraft. Their shortening of the distance between Europe and Asia equalled the significance of the Suez Canal. New airports became a basic infrastructure necessity. We in Singapore saw the pre-war Kallang airport replaced in 1955 by new facilities at Paya Lebar and gradually the old piston driven aircraft vanished from our skies.

I was to take advantage of this new international air travel with a number of flights out of Singapore, when either representing Singapore or as an academic with Southeast Asian credentials, I attended university-based conferences ranging from Tunis to Philadelphia, from Beirut to Montreal. One of the earliest was to Hong Kong in September 1961.

The Comet was the world's first commercial jet aircraft. It was then the darling of BOAC (British Overseas Aircraft Corporation). With its two Mark V Avon turbo jets it cruised at a comfortable 515 mph. As with the Gloster Meteor, the jet fighter, which I had seen while serving in the RAAF in England in 1944, here it seemed was Britain leading the way again. It was removed from service not long after our cruise to Hong Kong, design weaknesses having caused a number of fatal and for some time inexplicable crashes. One such victim was Chester Wilmot, Australian war correspondent and author of *The Struggle for Europe*, who with his brother-in-law Graham Irwin, my colleague, had dined with us some time before.

In those days you approached Kai Teck's airport's one and only runway, which jutted into the ocean, from the South China Sea. You then flew up "The Slot" as it was called, descending through more or less continuous cloud, with the tops of rather hilly islands appearing on either side of you. One, towering up — Hong Kong itself — was momentarily visible almost alongside, a little too close for comfort. It was necessary to touch down at the tip of the then rather stumpy (2,500 m) runway. Overshoot and you could crash into the airport buildings and crowded housing blocks waiting at the far end. Fall short to crash into the sea wall (as had happened with fatal results at Kallang in early 1954, shortly after I had arrived in Singapore) or you were in the drink. Fortunately we did neither but landed safely, to enjoy the ferry ride across to the island.

Hong Kong University was founded in 1911, at much the same time as was born the Republic of China. To commemorate its 50th anniversary, the colonial government struck a special issue of stamps, snapped up by philatelist enthusiasts such as me while the university itself organised an international symposium on the economic and social problems of "The Far East". Some 100 delegates flew in, courtesy of the Ford and Asia Foundations. Most were from the USA and the UK. There were several Japanese and a few from Taiwan. I was one of the six from Southeast Asia, while local bankers and entrepreneurs of various shapes and sizes came to listen and just possibly to learn.

It was a multi-disciplinary conference, with sociologists, economists, political scientists, lawyers (Zelman Cowan, Dean of Law at Melbourne University and later to be Australia's governor general, was one) as well as a few historians. It made for a most stimulating concourse, concerned very largely with China and the Chinese.

The overwhelming number of delegates from out of Asia gave it to me an old-fashioned air. It was almost as bizarre as a conference on the Problems of Western Europe filled largely with Chinese and Indians. Westerners discussing Asia, in Asia, with hardly an Asian present, however, reflected Hong Kong itself, where colonialism still was in control and the white man still ruled. Hong Kong, its ambience of the time described vividly by the first chapter in Han Suyin's *A Many Splendid Thing*, was an anachronism which I felt could not last much longer, and it jarred my Singapore sensitivities.

Nevertheless, now that Hong Kong has become again part of China, and the colonialists of that era continue to receive more than a scattering of abuse from Western and Eastern media and revisionist historians, it is salutary to recall the comments about the university, and Hong Kong itself, by Sun Yat Sen, the Chinese revolutionary and founder of the Chinese Republic in 1911.

Speaking to its students in 1923, and himself a medical graduate of the university, he said, "... I feel as though I had returned home because Hong Kong and its university are my intellectual birthplace. I have never before been able to answer the question properly but now I am in a position to answer it today. The question is 'Where did I get my revolutionary and modern ideas from?' The answer is I got them in this very place, in the Colony of Hong Kong. I compared Heung Shan, my native town, with Hong Kong, and although they are only 50 miles apart the difference in government oppressed me very much."

"Afterwards I saw the outside world and I began to wonder how it was that foreigners, that Englishmen would do such things as they have with the barren rock of Hong Kong within 70 or 80 years, while in 4,000 years China had no place like Hong Kong. My fellow students, you and I have studied in this English colony and in an English university. We must learn by English examples. We must carry this English example of good government to every part of China."

Well over a million refugees from the mainland had poured into Hong Kong since the communists had taken control a little over a decade before, very strongly confirming the teaching of Mencius, 2,000 years earlier: "Where government is good, it attracts, where it is not good it repels." Stuart Kirkby, professor of Economics at Hong Kong University and chairman of the conference, reminded me of Mencius and gave me Dr Sun's address when I naively compared Singapore's progress to independence with the *status quo* of Hong Kong. It made me reflect, what else could Hong Kong have done? It was training its own to fill every possible position, professional or otherwise, reserving only a handful of political power points until the handover in 1997. And when this came it had remained, in the terms Mencius had stated, a good government.

My paper at this conference was on the Chinese and the plural society they had created in Malaya. I argued that communism, then a major political and military menace on the peninsula, was not as long lasting a problem as communalism, that is the racialism endemic in Chinese-Malay relations. It was one of the 17 papers from the 50 discussed at the symposium that was chosen for publication in the magnificent book subsequently published by Hong Kong University Press. Its reasoning would appear to have stood the test of time. Fifty years on communism has gone but communalism remains. Chinese-Malay relations persist as a weakness at the heart of Malaysia.

The highlight of the next conference, held in Taipei, capital of Taiwan, in October 1962, was meeting Dr Sun's brother-in-law, Chiang Kai Shek. This was a very different gathering to that in Hong Kong. There the Westerner had dominated. Here, with again well over 100 delegates, all except two of us were Asians. Even the airline taking us across from Hong Kong, CAT (Civil Air Transport) was Chinese, with the interior of the old DC6 divided by red moon shaped arches. Taipei was crowded, concrete dust from new buildings thick in the air, unpleasant; but the conference, held in the huge Japanese built museum, most rewarding. It was sponsored by the International Association of Historians of Asia, IAHA, established by Filipino academics at a conference in Manila in 1960. I had sent a paper, being unable to attend, in March. In it I reiterated my view, already accepted in Singapore, calling for a new look at Asian history, where not the then dominant European version but Asia itself would be the subject of study. This was fairly heavy stuff at the time in Manila, almost, thought many Americans, subversive. It attracted media attention as well as academic support (as did my rejection of the Philippine claim to Sabah).

Partly because of this I was elected secretary-general of IAHA when the Taipei conference began. It had established branches in South Korea, Japan, Rykuyus, Taiwan, Vietnam, Hong Kong, Thailand, Malaya, Indonesia and Singapore. I was handed the files. Father Horacio de la Costa, the Jesuit historian (who later became the worldwide head of the Society in Rome) had preceded me. He put me wise to my election. The CIA, which funded us, was anxious to build up indigenous anti-communist but pro-nationalist organisations in Asia. It was necessary to have a spokesman from a country acceptable to all. Singapore, and my expressed views, filled the bill. Whatever the reason, I was honoured. The conference photo has me in the front row, serried ranks of Asians behind, Wang Shih-Cheih of Taiwan, Rong Syamananda of Bangkok, Domingo Abella and Horacio de la Costa of Manila, Yoshihiko Teruya from Kyoto alongside me, all of us beaming away. We related very amicably to each other and lasting friendships were formed there, while the IAHA and its conferences in Asia continue to this day.

On that first day, October 6, we were all in our best suits. Inside a large hall our seats had been moved back to the side. In the empty space near the far end was one magnificent chair. Nervously we waited. Wang Shih-Cheih was outside, at the bottom of the broad sweep of steps that led down to the drive. We heard police sirens as a cavalcade of cars drew up. Some security men entered. We rose to our feet. The Chinese bowed low.

Chiang Kai Shek (or Jiang Jie-Shi as he is called now) was then 75 years old. He once had ruled China. His life of struggle and success, and that of his party the Kuo Min Tang, had been inseparably linked to the mainland. One of the great men of the world in the first half of the 20th century, defeated by Mao Tse Tung, another colossus in Asian history, he now presided over a dynamic entrepreneurial state, its agrarian reforms unique in Asia, its economic growth rate the envy of the world, its hatred of the Communists buttressed by very visible signs of US military assistance. We looked at this withered, skinny yet somehow patrician leader with awe.

The premier Chen Cheng and the Minister of Education Huang Chi stood behind him as from the ornate throne-chair he read us a speech. "I have personally experienced the modern historical developments in my country", he said in something of an understatement, and he spoke of the dangers of communism coming to power in other Asian countries. We were warned to combat this in whatever way we could. He was optimistic. In the long future, "freedom will overcome slavery, light vanquish darkness", provided we worked together. An English translation was handed to us within minutes of his conclusion.

We applauded standing. The old man was escorted to a side room. We relaxed in groups, reading his speech, discussing the man and the event. A Chinese approached me. As secretary-general, I was to meet the generalissimo. Wang Shih-Cheih, a tubby little man, introduced me as I bowed, and translated, "You come from Singapore? Many Chinese in Singapore", he told me. I replied "Yes, Your Excellency, mainly Hokkien, sturdy workers. And it had the honour once to welcome your predecessor and colleague, Dr Sun Yat Sen." His rather impassive — or was it bored? — face broke into an interested glance at me. "That was many years ago. A great man, founder of our Party and our modern nation." I was on the point of saying that Mao and the CCP had the same view. I thought better of it. His was not a kind face. I doubt if we shared the same sense of humour. "Mr Lee Kuan Yew is our leader now. We all have great respect for him." "Yes, he is a good man who can handle the communist pariahs." Praise from this right wing relic was the last thing Lee Kuan Yew, then endeavouring to be more left than his near rivals, would have valued. I kept this comment to myself.

Manila and Macapagal come next. In 1962 an adroitly worded application had resulted in a Carnegie Fellowship. This enabled me to tour the USA early the following year on a three-month lecture program at those American universities with interests in Southeast Asia. It began when flying east to the East-West Centre in Hawaii, I stopped in Manila to spend several days at the Ateneo de Manila, the venerable Jesuit College, with my friend Fr Horacio de la Costa, my host.

Coming from Singapore I found the Philippines another world. It was hardly part of Southeast Asia, rather it was Central America with a Yankee accent. The Iberian colonial culture which for four hundred years had impregnated these islands had left entrenched a wealthy ruling class and an authoritarian church, an elite indifferent to their urban and landless rural poor, whose language they little learned, an attitude similar to the relationship between the hidalgos and mestizos in their Mexican haciendas and the peons. Whereas in Central and South America however it took over 100 years after Spanish-Portuguese rule was overthrown before democratic civilian government became more than a passing fad, here in the Philippines a superficial democracy rushed in with the Americans at the beginning of the 20th century; but with the Iberian culture flourishing beneath this thin veneer. So it is today.

For over a decade I had studied and lectured on its history. There seemed little holding this pastiche of islands and cultures together. Comparisons with the states of Central or South America seemed more valid than comparisons with the states of Southeast Asia. Indeed the academics and politicians regarded their country more as a stepping stone or bridge between East and West than as another Southeast Asian nation. I could not accept this highly self-laudatory view. I found its people extravagant, emotional and charming. Tales of corruption were commonplace, so too incidents of violent crime. In the south, in the Sulu archipelago, where Islam reigned, the grip of Manila was weak, as it always had been, from the time of the Spanish occupation, where each night in Jolo, so W.L. Pryer, the founder of Sandakan reported in 1879, "the Spanish sentries nervously cry 'Alerte'". Their descendants behave much the same today, and as effectively.

A few years earlier the Republic had made official what I regarded as absurdly unrealistic claims for the "return" of North Borneo. It belonged to the Philippines, said the President. Ceded to the British in the 19th century by the then Sultan of Sulu, who surrendered in totality his extremely dubious rights over the east coast rivers, and a cession accepted by Spain, his nominal over-lord, North Borneo for nigh on 100 years had been administered, in a manner acceptable to all, by a handful of British officers and their assistants.

I had studied the original documents concerning this cession, as well as all the official despatches at the Foreign Office, and the ensuing international treaties of the powers concerned, such as Spain, Britain, the Colonial US administration and the indepen-dent Republic of the Philippines. In several books and academic journals I had pointed to the baselessness of the claim. Not one iota of evidence could be produced that Sabah was not British and was soon to be part of Malaysia. Ah! Malaysia! Was this the underlying reason for the claim?

It was pursued with such vigour from 1960 on that both the British and then the Malaysian governments were concerned, and felt the need to respond. My articles, as well as the original documents concerning the cession were studied, and gradually the tub-thumping and extravagant claims died away. To me it was just one illustration of the excesses, the lack of international maturity of this Manila government.

My experience there added to this impression. A visit to its legislature with its prominent notice "No personal firearms past this sign" was disconcerting to say the least. Later several of my academic friends assured me this was never enforced, but that no shots had been fired in the chamber for some years, so no-one worried. They all carried a pistol, but more as a macho symbol than anything else.

A stroll along the waterfront Roxas Boulevard with an American friend after a rather effusive dinner was equally disconcerting. A few stops behind us walked an armed sentry who left the entrance of some building we had passed, to follow us, his rifle clearly focused on our backs. We cut short our walk.

Manila, founded in 1571, was full of beggars, more than I had seen in a decade elsewhere in Southeast Asia. For this the Roman Catholic Church, with its adamant opposition to family planning, was largely to blame. And there was Malacanang Palace. With two leading Filipino historians I was to present to President Macapagal a gift from the International Association of Historians of Asia, 55 volumes of records relating to his country from 1493 AD onwards. This rare collection, published in 1898, put together by Blair and Robertson, was virtually unobtainable. We had taken it to Taipei where a "pirated" copy of it had been produced — Taiwan not being a signature of the Geneva International Copyright agreement — and it was our way of saying thank you for the assistance given by the Philippine government to the IAHA.

Macapagal received us warmly, but it was obvious as he stared blankly at the trolley of books he had not the faintest idea what the gift was, what it signified, what he was supposed to say to us. Clearly he had received no briefing on the appointment. It was a fiasco. "If you do not want them I would love them" was on the tip of my tongue, but instead I was pushed forward as the historian who denied the Philippines its rightful "reoccupation" of North Borneo. Macapagal was urbane enough to laugh this off; and offer us all some refreshment. We walked out onto the broad first floor veranda. Here a rather flashy coca-cola self-serve machine had "Out of Order" slapped across it. Fish go rotten from the head down. I was not that surprised when Marcos succeeded him.

Tibetan jewellery bought from refugees in Connaught Place and five Rajasthan dolls were my gifts when I returned home from a conference in Delhi. The Congress of Orientalists, formed in Paris in 1876, held here its first ever gathering in Asia, in January 1964. Ample funds, mainly from American Foundations, enabled several thousand scholars and charlatans from all over Asia, but particularly India, to meet with savants from Europe and the USA during a week of junkets and deliberations.

On arrival at Delhi's Param International Airport there had been some confusion. No Tregonning was listed as a delegate. A harassed Congress clerk unavailingly scanned page after page as scores of newly arrived academics were seized by excited students and ferried away to their pre-arranged accommodation. I remained a non-person.

Several flurried hours later it was agreed I go into Delhi — a room at its most expensive hotel, the Ashoka, was found for me — and I would check again next morning at the Congress head-quarters. So into the night I plunged. Next morning a painstaking search of the Congress Lists revealed a KGT Raffles, professor of history at the University of Singapore. I was safe! I kept the metal name tag I was given and wore it with pride. This was lucky for it led to a fortunate meeting a week later.

On the first afternoon of the Congress we were the guests of the President of the Republic, Rajagopalachan, at a reception at Rashtrepati Bhavan, the President's official residence. We entered the magnificent building designed by Sir Edwin Lutyens for the British Viceroy, and passed through it to the Mughal gardens beyond. At the intersection of wide paths that led between lawns and flower beds stood members of the President's bodyguard. Motionless, fierce of visage, in black and gold head-dress, red jacket with gold belt, white breeches and black knee high boots, a gauntleted hand holding rigid a lance with a red and white pennant fluttering from it, each guard looked eight feet tall. They made the guards at Buckingham Palace seem inconsequential by comparison.

Suddenly from the long window behind us there was a sus-tained trumpet fanfare. Out from the palace emerged the President of India with Professor Humayun Kabir, the President of our Congress. They walked slowly down the broad path. As each bodyguard was passed he fell in behind. By the time the President of the Republic mounted a small dais near the middle of the gardens the line of giants behind him was some 20 or more. They swung around and faced us. The world's most stirring national anthem, Tagore's proud "Jai Hind" burst forth and lifted us up. It was a brilliant moment.

Munching a cucumber sandwich later, Stuart Kirkby of Hong Kong told me the whole procedure (excluding Tagore) had echoed the pre-war vice regal gathering, even to the cucumbers. Nevertheless the occasion and the surrounding had been evocative of a great country not too proud to honour foreign scholarship and not too obsessed with a new nationalism to forget its great Mughal days either.

Although its roots lie deep in antiquity, and it was a famous city before Alexander reached the Indus River, Delhi is essentially a Mughal city. Outstanding is the Red Fort, the greatest of all Mughal Palaces, built by Shah Jahan between 1639 and 1648. Indian friends slipped me into the courtyard of the nearby Jama Masjid, one of Asia's greatest mosques, built by Shah Jahan in 1650 and took me far up Chandi Chowk, the most crowded bazaar imaginable. At Agra other friends showed me over not only the Taj Mahal, but also where Shah Jahan, imprisoned in the Agra Fort built by his grandfather Akbar, would lie, looking across the river to where his masterpiece was nearing completion, an exquisite memory of his love, his wife Arjumand Bano Begum.

The Samadhi and the Rajghat, the peaceful garden by the river where in 1948 Mahatma Ghandi's body was laid on the funeral pyre and burnt before perhaps a million people, was another highlight; but overshadowing all else was a chance encounter on our final day.

He came almost unannounced. It was not in our program; I suspect he substituted for a lesser dignitary. Nearly all Europeans were elsewhere, I was with my friend Dr Vishnal Singh of the Indian School of International Studies (Sapru House) which had just offered me a Visiting Professorship. Several of my friends from Manila, Kuala Lumpur, Calcutta were also there. And then Nehru began talking.

Much of the rhetoric of opening speeches and presidential addresses had stressed the value of Oriental Studies in helping the West understand the East. Nehru in contrast called on the East to understand itself. He deplored the colonial system (under which he had been educated) that had given him little knowledge or understanding of other parts of Asia. (And of course I had seen this same failing in Singapore.) Two years before, in 1962, when Chinese armies had swept down the Tibetan valleys into India, and when he was striving to establish contact with Beijing, he said that India had fewer than half a dozen scholars with graduate qualifications in Chinese. There were thousands who could speak French or German, but the languages of Asia were hardly known.

India, he said, lacked the cultural conditions that had bred in the Chinese a contempt for the outside world. India had the curiosity and tolerance to study Asia, while at the same time developing an ever richer technological and scientific knowledge of the West. He hoped that all Asians listening to him would go home aware they were part of a great continent and with European dominance in decline, an Asian century was beginning.

With a mass of Indians I crowded forward to the steps from the stage, down which he carefully came. Slim, tired, his famous rose in his lapel, he was helped to a side door. He stopped to greet a friend, and saw me the only European in the hall. He had me brought through. I greeted him Indian fashion, he gave me a gentle hand. I remember its touch today.

He read my stupid label "KGT Raffles, Professor of History, Singapore", and asked, "are you related to the Raffles who went from Calcutta to found your great city?" So I told him of the mistake and while doing so he motioned to a divan and we sat together. He asked with a smile whether I was one of the culprits who taught colonial history or British history only, and I was able to reply that we stood in Asia, and had several strong courses, including one in which his letters from prison, written to his daughter, were studied; and another in which India's great influence on Southeast Asia in the early millennia was a key element.

He was delighted, a charming smile, "Good, good. One day when I have time I must visit again Southeast Asia." "Oh yes,"

I replied, "and bring your daughter with you." We both smiled again, he was helped to his feet, and he passed on.

Here was a great man, perhaps in terms of sheer achievement India's greatest man of the 20th century, the leader who had led it to independence. His curiosity and courtesy, his unobtrusive mixing with his followers were in marked contrast to other leaders I had met. I mourned his death a few months later in May 1964, and accepted with pride the subsequent invitation from the Indian Council for Cultural Relations to be a nominator for the Jawaharlal Nehru Award for International Understanding. This, the Asian equivalent of the Nobel Prize (of which also as a strange coincidence I was a nominator), clearly called for Asians alone to be considered.

The advice Nehru offered remains relevant. Asian nations desperately need to tolerate each other. Disputes between India and Pakistan, China and Japan, the nations that are neighbours in Southeast Asia, those on the high plateau of central Asia, their quarrels can no longer be blamed on the West. Basically, as Nehru said in his beautiful voice, the problems of Asia are for Asians themselves to solve. And surely this understanding begins in the classrooms of the continent?

One of the poems that I read those days to my children in the evening before they trundled upstairs to bed was *Madeline*, where Miss Clovell sat up, turned on the light and said, "Something is not quite right." Maybe it is not read to children anymore, charming though it is, but for us it signifies a special moment in their lives; my daughters now in the 40s and 50s, can still recite it.

My visit to Cambodia produced the same feeling; that something was not quite right. It had all began in the City Book Store, where I occasionally browsed, while my children unconcernedly wandered in the maze of open shops of Change Alley alongside, on Collyer Quay. One day the manager, a Mr Chen, told me of the new cheap airfares being offered for group travel. He suggested we form such a group and fly to London. With me at the time was Hugh Tinker, author and scholar of Southeast Asia, from the School of Oriental and African Studies in London, whose son was later killed in the Falklands war. He suggested a Singapore branch of the Royal Institute of International Affairs. I wrote to Arnold Toynbee, the director, who had called on me some years before and this was arranged; but somehow it all moved away from me into Singapore hands — which in all my enterprises I had encouraged anyway — and we were going not to the UK but to Cambodia. This was much more exciting.

As a member of a miscellaneous group of Europeans and Asians in November 1965, I flew there in an ancient DC6 of Royal Air Cambodge. Police motorcyclists, sirens blaring, escorted our coach taking us from the airport to our hotel in Phnom Penh. Cheering, clapping crowds of people welcomed at each street corner. In some consternation we hurriedly moved all our Asian friends to the window seats. Here, while we tried to disappear, they waved to acknowledge this unexpected welcome, as traffic police stopped other traffic to give us a free flow across every intersection.

We thought it all a mistake, for we were no official delegation, indeed little more than a band of quasi-tourists; or so I thought.

That evening however, our coach took us to an official reception and buffet dinner, hosted by Son Sann, the Vice President of the committee of ministers, two other ministers in Samreth Soth and Nguon Chhay Kny, and other high dignitaries. Our leader was George Thomson, a long serving Singapore civil servant. Fortunately his French was sufficiently fluent to toast the Head of State, Prince Norodom Sihanouk in reply to one given by our hosts, to Singapore's Prime Minister, Lee Kuan Yew.

Some of our party, apprehensive at the rumour that only French was spoken were delighted to discover this was not so. "There's any number of them who speak Hokkien," Mr Chen told me. The mutual admiration party *dans une atmosphere très cordiale* as the local press observed, concluded at midnight, with George deep in discussion with Son Sann.

Next day we were received at the palace by the Head of State, Prince Norodom Sihanouk. He came to meet us, greeting us half way into the long audience hall, bubbling and cheerful, procedure and court etiquette swept aside. He gave us a most frank interview, in idiomatic English easily comprehended.

Crowned king in 1941 at the age of 18, and ignored by his French master, he was unable to stop the rapacious Thais from annexing the western province of his country, but with the end of Japanese occupation and French withdrawal he secured the independence of Cambodia in 1953, at much the same time as we had arrived in Singapore. In 1955 he abdicated, was elected Head of State five years later. Throughout he had guided Cambodia with a skill and political astuteness that resembled Lee in Singapore, "to whom," he asked George Thomson, "please convey my warmest best wishes."

The problems of his lovely land were many. Help in overcoming these would be welcome. On the international scene he saw a communist victory in Vietnam as inevitable. He hated the communists but he was too close to the Vietnam fire-storm to take sides; and he could not see the USA as a long time ally. He was "a small gecko between two wild elephants", said Sihanouk. He wished to maintain Cambodia's neutral independent position. He hoped Singapore would support him.

He told us of his country's weak infrastructure. The French had regarded Cambodia, against all its history, its millennia of fear and hatred of the Vietnamese, as part of French Indo-China; and Indo-China as part of the economy of France. No Cambodians had been trained — there was not one Khmer doctor on independence in 1953, and only two schools for six million people. All clerical and administrative posts, no matter how minor, had been reserved for Frenchmen; even the gendarmes came from Toulouse "All we had," he said with a wry smile, "were ruins."

We saw these ruins a few days later. Angkor is one of the great wonders of the world. I had read much about it, its history, its "discovery" by Henri Mouhot in 1861, its art, and indeed from 1953 onwards had lectured on it to my students. Initially none of them knew of its existence although well aware of St. Peter's

Cathedral in Rome and Westminster Abbey in London. Thus does colonialism emasculate culture. Yet although I knew it well I found the power and mystery of its jungle-clad temples overwhelming.

We stayed in a Chinese-run hotel in the nearby village of Siem Reap. In a pedi-cab (*kong dups* they are called) peddled by a cheerful Khmer youth, I would set off in the freshness of dawn. Squawking jungle birds, chattering and coughing monkeys, buffalo bells and kingfishers diving into the broad lily covered moat accompanied me as I explored the Bayon, several other but more ruined temples long abandoned and given over to the jungle, but in particular Angkor Wat itself.

It had remained a place of Buddhist worship after the 15th-century sacking of the vast complex, with a small community of monks keeping the jungle at bay. There it stood, this magnificent 12th-century temple, the largest religious monument in the world, its perfect symmetry a masterpiece of architectural genius and a sublime work of sacred art. I climbed over it with awe.

On several occasions I was with some of the Singapore group escorted by small Khmer children as "guides", one who offered me his sister for a few dollars, but often I was on my own. Angkor was just coming to be recognised as a reachable world wonder, but there were few other visitors. At Bantrei Srei, some 20 kilometres away, where we admired this exquisite miniature complex, we were on our own. It was there that our Khmer driver glancing nervously around told us in whispered apprehension of "le Khmer Rouge". We thought of them as comparable to our Malayan CTs, never for a moment anticipating the horror they represented and which a decade later, in a fanaticism that surpassed that of Auschwitz, was to murder a million of these charming people.

One evening a small group of the Royal Cambodian Ballet, led by Sihanouk's daughter Princess Buppha Devi, danced for us on the parvis in front of Angkor Wat. It was an incomparable setting, strong arc lights across the moat, the temple towering behind, the colour and grace of the dancers enjoyed by all the villagers of Siem Reap who sat enraptured throughout that warm evening;

as did Sihanouk himself, making a most unexpected visit to join George Thomson on the temporary bamboo stand erected for us.

Angkor, I thought represented the quintessence of Southeast Asia, and how arrogant was the Western claim that it had been "discovered" in 1861. It had nothing to do with Europe, it far surpassed anything that civilisation had produced, and the enigmatic and mystical atmosphere that permeated the temple in its verdant setting crowded my memory as we returned.

But there was also the perplexing mystery as to our reception and the involvement of the Prince, the Head of State. I came to suspect it was allied to the tense political struggle that year, 1965, in Malaysia. In May at UMNO's general assembly a resolution had been unanimously passed demanding the arrest and detention of Lee Kuan Yew. Ismail, the Minister for Home Affairs, said that month, "if Mr Lee uses force, I'll put him in detention". Lee himself was visiting Laos. On his return he said, "if we must have trouble, let us have it now instead of waiting for another five or ten years".

John Drysdale's well-documented *Singapore: Struggle For Success*, in its comments on the strong possibility of Malaysia taking arbitrary measures to block Lee's move for a Malaysian Malaysia, refers to his possible arrest and Singapore's fallback plans should this eventuate. Apparently preparations in 1965 were under way for a Singapore Government-in-Exile to be established in Cambodia, led by Lee's long-time lieutenant, S. Rajaratnam.

My suspicion is that our visit, led by George Thomson, most trustworthy confidant of Mr Lee and faithful servant of Singapore's government, was part of this. Certainly the Singapore branch of the Royal Institute of International Affairs vanished from the scene. Presumably its purpose had been served. And although he never once mentioned it, the bookshop manager who had first suggested the idea, Mr Chen, turned out I believe to be the brother of Linda Chen, once the interpreter for Lee Kuan Yew. As we know, Mr Lee, to me perhaps one of the greatest Asians of the 20th century, was not arrested; rather Singapore was ejected from Malaysia while Cambodia disappeared from the civilised world. As for me, I flew back with a bad dose of dengue fever: not recommended.

The last international conference I attended was in Tokyo, which gave me an unexpected bonus. Organised by the Japanese Centre for East Asian Cultural Studies and UNESCO, a small group of us — one representative each from Korea, Vietnam, the Philippines, Indonesia, Thailand, China (Taiwan), Malaysia and Singapore — with an equal number of Japanese — met in October 1966 to discuss East Asia's differing responses to Western Culture. For my sins, as the only non-Asian, I was made rapporteur of the conference. It was a fascinating experience.

A reception was held for us at the Mitsui Club, in the head-quarters of this historic conglomerate. I was taken to meet an elderly guest. Wearing a classic grey robe, on which I recognised with a start of surprise the famous hollyhock crest on his left sleeve, was a slight, bespectacled Japanese with an unmistakeable aura of dignity about him. "Selamat malam" (good afternoon) he said as he shook my hand, his eyes twinkling. This was the 80-year-old Marquis Yoshichika Tokugawa, the 5th son of the last shogun, Shungaku Tokugawa, who as a 25 year old in 1853 had witnessed the arrival in Yedo Bay of Commodore Perry of the USN on his mission to open Japan to the world. The Tokugawa clan had ruled Japan as Shoguns since Ieyasu in 1603. It was a rare privilege to meet the descendant of such a famous family.

He and his son Yoshitomo, who stood beside the old man, were anxious to talk of Malaya, where the father had been a tree-hugger or arborial botanist since his first visit in 1921. To my astonishment this gentle scholar congratulated me on being a Vice President of the MBRAS whose journal he had long read. They were sent to him by his friend, the Sultan of Johor.

Hostile to the paramountcy of the military in Japan's affairs, his opposition expressed in the House of Peers had sidelined him from any public activity. This little appealed to him anyway, he was happiest as a research botanist and in developing a Tokugawa museum in Nagoya. He shared a love of nature with the emperor, and was appointed director of the Raffles Museum and Singapore's Botanical Gardens 1942–44. Here with cool disdain he sheltered — hid perhaps a better word — several British botanists and marine biologists, who worked with him during the Syonan years to collect and preserve the scientific collections of the Gardens, and the thousands of books and the invaluable items of the museum.

Ordered by the military to destroy the statue of Raffles that was a feature of the port, he had it taken down, then kept it in the museum. This was but one of many subtle acts of bravery he performed in a period of extreme difficulty for all concerned. So too Yoshitomo who had been mayor of Johor Bahru, then in 1944 in charge of the P.O.W. camp in Tokyo. When I spoke to him he was Vice President of the British-Japan Society and had been awarded by the Queen the British Empire Order of the CBE.

On their gentle advice the next afternoon it was arranged for me to visit the Toyo Bunko, the wonderful library of east and central Asia, a unique collection amassed by the Australian G.E. Morrison, "Morrison of Peking", during his years as The Times correspondent there during the tumultuous years of the Boxer revolt and the birth of the Republic. The director of the institute who showed me around, Dr Hirosato Iwai treated me with such respect and courtesy that clearly the Tokugawa advice had reached him.

The Marquis also had pointed me towards Nikko, in the mountains behind Tokyo. Here was the shrine for Ieyasu Tokugawa, the founder of the shogun dynasty in the early 17th century, and much more of great beauty all steeped in Japanese history and culture. A cherished weekend on which I reflected on my return to Singapore. What a contrast between those who had decapitated my school friend shot down over New Guinea, or those who had cold bloodedly massacred thousands of Chinese in Singapore, and this gentleman epitomising a unique culture, carrying such a famous name that even today telling my Japanese acquaintances that "I have talked to a Tokugawa" brings me a bow and a hiss of appreciation.

Other conferences, in Kuala Lumpur, Beirut, Hawaii, Philadelphia, Montreal and Canberra, where I argued with the Australian Foreign Affairs Minister, Senator Barwick, fade in my memory, while I recall this gentle man with the famous name with continued affection.

10 Lee Kuan Yew

I t had been just another day at work — actually it was August 9, 1965 — when my colleague and friend Sharom Ahmat came into my room. "You had better not go into town today, prof., there might be trouble." "How come?" I asked. "We've just been chucked out of Malaysia and there could be a riot." And later we watched on TV as our Premier, Lee Kuan Yew, with anguish in his voice and tears in his eyes told us that the goal of his life and that of so many others was now but an impossible dream. Singapore, which had been part of Malaysia since September 1963, had been evicted in a political move unprecedented in history.

Yet there were no riots, rather an overwhelming sense of relief. Somehow, thought many of us, we could be better off on our own. It had been a difficult merger with Malaysia. The rights and wrongs of the various disputes will be long debated. Both sides were at fault, perhaps, in not seeking equitable compromises. Perhaps it was never a possibility, with differences wider than those that precipitated the American civil war. Who can tell now?

Clearly a multiracial port city with a pent up entrepreneurial dynamism in its migrant people had fitted uncomfortably into a country with centuries of Malay cultural and renewed political dominance and a laid back lifestyle. The hierarchal social structure of Malaysia jarred the egalitarian outlook of Singapore, and vice versa. Challenges to that political dominance, in particular, produced increasing resentment and concern.

There had been, in July 1964, Singapore's first ever Sino-Malay riot, with 22 people killed and hundreds injured before order was restored. Sharom had been thinking of this when he warned me to stay on the campus. Yet even after that riot merger with Malaysia still seemed the only way in which the future of Singapore could be assured. The only alternative, scarcely considered, as the British relinquished their last vestiges of colonial control and prepared to wind down their naval base, was the forbidding prospect of going it alone. Now that prospect had become a reality. I was present at the birth of another nation, yet another merdeka. It was an emotional moment and my heart went out to Lee Kuan Yew, in whom lay all our hopes for the future.

As the years of struggle against the communists from 1954 onwards had produced a gradual movement by Mr Lee towards the previously-scorned English-speaking intellectuals; Parkinson once induced him into speaking to his evening gathering. (It was not a success.) He several times addressed the staff as a whole and ever more warmly won their support. He was still regarded by us however as a man not to be trifled with. He suffered fools not gladly and as many of us felt foolish in his presence it was often less than an enjoyable experience. Tales of him sacking civil servants who turned up late for work, of his puritanical attitude to any suggestion of corruption, of his stern standards for public and private behaviour were commonplace.

For some obscure reason, I think because as an expatriate I was one of an endangered species, I had been elected President of the staff association. I recall one meeting in particular. The government had been nasty to us, our Vice-chancellor seemed too compliant for our liking, and the lecture theatre, crowded with disgruntled staff, felt that the President should wait on the Prime Minister. No, he's an expatriate, a local should go, a deputation perhaps. There was an immediate backsliding. No, that would cause the President to lose face (actually that would not have worried me) but no, a deputation of all Faculties should go, no, it had to be the President. The arguments raged on with no decision taken. I maintained a discreet silence. The Vice President, an eminent Chinese surgeon, quietly turned on what in those days we called a transistor radio, which he had in his breast pocket. "Good heavens," he said, "they are racing." It was Saturday afternoon, and the Bukit Timah race meeting was under way. He left in a hurry to place his bet, followed by most of the Chinese in the theatre. The Tamil is a litigacious individual but even he tried. I suggested to the weary remainder that I seek the advice of our Chancellor, the former British High Commissioner Malcolm McDonald. All agreed. He was in India and by the time he replied the issue was dead. My meeting with Mr Lee was left to another day, to a more propitious occasion altogether.

It was also totally unexpected. "The Prime Minister's press secretary," said the voice on the phone. "Mr Lee would like to see you at 9 a.m. tomorrow."

I answered the summons with some nervousness. I recalled the experience of Lea Sheridan. The university had established a Law Faculty, and Lea Sheridan, its new professor, had recently arrived from England. The local legal fraternity had acquired their degrees (as had Mr Lee) in London. They were jealous of their exclusive control of the profession, and with the conservatism characteristic of their profession were maintaining that they would recognise only lawyers trained in the UK.

Sheridan waited on the Minister of Law, and immaculate in his new tropical suit, was met by a PAP stalwart in the white slacks and open neck shirt of a true member of the proletariat. The interview was less than cordial. Suitably admonished, Sheridan next day called on the Prime Minister. This time to demonstrate his affinity to this independent nation he was tie less and in white slacks. Mr Lee, immaculate in tropical suit, greeted him with a scowl: "do you always call on prime ministers in such casual clothes?" Despite this, the local degree was recognised; but it had been a disconcerting experience for Sheridan. He left soon after for the peace and quiet of Belfast in Northern Ireland.

So what should I wear was more of a problem than what the PM wanted of me. Clothes in Asia conveyed a political message

then, perhaps less so today although there is still some significance to what is worn by the leaders, however subtle the signal.
Carefully I climbed the steps of the former City Hall, where in
turn Yamashita and Mountbatten had reviewed their victorious
troops, and went to the second floor where the PM had his office.
I wore well pressed slacks, a long sleeved shirt and a tie; and
passed muster.

Armed police stood at each landing. After my appointment had
been checked a door was unlocked. I waited in a small window-
less but air-conditioned room. Here I was met by the press
secretary to the PM. He unlocked an inner door and took me
into the Conference or Cabinet Room, a much more spacious
place altogether. We waited to be summoned by the PM.

Lee Kuan Yew is not a Hokkien, as are most of the Chinese in
Singapore, but a Hakka, a small rather maligned South Chinese
people, secretive and by repute long time Triad supporters. When
he and his fellow activists formed the PAP, he could not speak
to his countrymen face to face other than in English or Malay.
The press secretary told me how Mr Lee became fluent in both
Mandarin and Hokkien during his years of leadership. It was
a remarkable achievement of intellect and willpower, lessons
crowded in whenever he had a spare moment, particularly when
you consider the intense daily political struggle which in those
years occupied the full-time involvement of this remarkable man.

I had met the press secretary some years before, at the
Nanyang, or South Seas, Society, a group of Chinese-educated
Singaporeans interested in the study of the Chinese in Southeast
Asia. I had been taken there by Victor Purcell, former Malayan
civil servant and a scholarly pioneer in the field. We shared an
interest in the Southeast Asian activities of the revolutionary Dr
Sun Yat Sen and of Kang Yu Wei, the great Chinese reformer, in
the 1900–10 period. Sun, the revolutionary, had lived for a time
on Tai Jin Road, quite close to the City Chambers, where we were
sitting, while raising funds for the revolutionaries in China.

We were discussing Kang Yu Wei when we were motioned into
the prime minister's office. Fortunately he was dressed much as

92

I was, in a thin tropical jacket, tie-less. He growled, "Lock the door; you know those police grow sleepy, we don't want someone bursting through." Indonesia was visible from the window, there were Indonesian agents in town as well as Malay extremists. Three separate attempts at assassination already had been foiled. His elimination was desired by many. Security was tight.

For over an hour he spoke to me, "I like what you have written about Singapore, Tregonning, I like your attitude. I think I can use some of your phrases", then dismissing me while he showered as I consulted a number of files. He had called me in, so I discovered, as a substitute for the Singapore correspondent of the influential Australian weekly, *The Bulletin*. It had failed, so the PM said, to describe accurately the government's underlying position and attitudes to Malaysia, the USA and the UK. He wanted no misunderstandings, and in various ways was attempting to set the record straight. Relations in particular with Malaysia were strained, and could deteriorate further. The editor of *The Bulletin*, Donald Horne, was waiting on me; so get to work!

That afternoon I wrote the first of several long articles and sent it off to Melbourne. I have to hope it helped in some small way. In retrospect what struck me most was not the frankness in which this dynamic man talked of matters confidential, but the trust he showed in me; for there was no suggestion I submit my copy to him or the press secretary, and it was clear that once I had been selected to do a particular job it was expected I would do it, while he turned to matters of more moment. A minor incident no doubt, but memorable to the participant: You don't often brush the sleeve of greatness.

Not long after — my diary reminds me it was July 7, 1966 — we were invited by Mr Lee to dinner at Sri Temasek to meet Dennis Healey, British Labour Party foreign affairs spokesman. The conversation which I captured reflects the climate of the time, now a forgotten world but real enough then. The war in Malaysia had calmed down markedly, all signs pointed to the retreat of the MCP and its remnants regrouping in Southern Thailand. Our long held fear that the MCP would receive support from a communist

Vietnam (or China) had weakened considerably, thanks to a decade long involvement of US forces based in Saigon. Their efforts, often maligned, had given us a much needed breathing space.

Healey was of the mind that communist infiltration into the democratically created infrastructure of the new nations of Malaysia and Singapore would become more of a danger than any military aid or foreign "volunteer" troops from overseas. He said to my Prime Minister, "We are agreed, I am sure, that China would never send its armies into Southeast Asia, but I for one do not rule out the possibility of it infiltrating and assisting the communist Parties of the region. That remains, to me, a serious possibility, which SEATO could not handle."

Mr Lee, as usual, was strong in his reply, "Firstly China, as with all other Lenin indoctrinated countries opposes on ideo-logical grounds sending troops across its borders unless — as happened in Korea — those borders appear threatened. However should friendly proletariat forces struggling against feudal ele-ments — as the jargon goes — should these forces ask for aid, it is perfectly correct to send volunteers. There are several recent examples of this. But I sense a change in China, a more pragmatic approach to international relations giving hope for better rela-tions all round. China after all is a nation and I see its national concerns — not international — as paramount. The communist Parties in Southeast Asia I sense will be left to wither on the vine. So too SEATO." And that is how it turned out.

I regard him still as one of the greatest leaders of Asia in all its history. For the first time ever, he more than anyone, had created a dynamic nation on the equator. For the first time ever he had the Chinese, despite their thousands of years of acceptance of political despotism as the only form of government suitable for the Middle Kingdom, taking part in a democracy; and very largely, despite the heavy weight of their ancestral culture, with its indifference to, or contempt of other cultures, had the Singapore Chinese embracing the English language and by this had them plugged into the outside world. All this, and much more, while we watched. It had been a unique experience. Even today I think the magnitude of his achievement is little recognised.

All this was still in process when we met (not for the last time) but already the enrolments at the massive Chinese language schools were crumbling as each year more and more parents sent their children to the English language schools, while an ever increasing number competed for admittance to our expanding university. By now Mr Lee, and the government generally, were turning to us for the much needed support required to develop a non-communist, non-colonial state. All over the world emerging nation-states were demonstrating that their survival and success depended above all on an educated hardworking indigenous middle class. In Singapore's case in this our alumni played a vital role.

Malaya or Malaysia as it was to become, also benefitted from the service of many of our early graduates. They were to prove the falsity of the wide-spread belief among locals as well as the expatriates of that time that the new country would collapse with the latter's departure: an inferiority complex writ large which we helped to demolish.

Unlike the Singapore contemporaries we (that is the university) contributed (to the best of my knowledge) only two politicians to the peninsula: Musa Hitam and a former medical student Dr Mahathir Mohamad. The latter was to become world famous as Malaysia's Prime Minister, while Musa's career, which began on campus as President of the student Democratic Club and ended rather controversially after a stint as Deputy Prime Minister, is yet to be recorded. He left an indelible impression on those who knew him.

We produced two distinguished historians from that early period — Khoo Kay Kim, later professor at the University in Kuala Lumpur, and J. Kathirithamby-Wells — and there were other scholars as well, such as Wang Gungwu, Hamzah Sendut, later Vice-chancellor in Penang, but the majority of graduates from our department made their mark in the civil service and subsequently in business.

I recall but a few, helped by glancing at a faded photo of the 1954 peninsula students who came to our flat on the top floor of the University's Wolverton Mess in Dalvey Road one evening. Malays abstain from alcohol and *kechil makan* is easily prepared, so such a gathering is never expensive. It was to be the first of many such cheery occasions.

There is Ungku Ubaidillah (later a *dato*, Director General Malaysian Fisheries Department), Matthew Mattai (Director General, Inland Revenue), Rajah Iskander (Director of Broadcasting), B. Nithianathan (Labour Commissioner) and Aputhnan Nelson (as a *dato*, senior positions in Malaysian Foreign Service). Many were involved in education including — Joginder Singh Jessy who retired as Principal of the prestigious Sultan Hamid College where Dr Mahathir had studied and where many years before Joginder — Dr Mahathir's father was Principal. Krishnan Iyer became headmaster of the Penang Free School, while Arulsothy was headmistress of a large secondary school in Kuala Lumpur. Hashim Aman rose to the top as chief secretary of the Malaysian Civil Service. These are but a few of those I recall.

I like to think of these students, along with their Singapore friends, as a rather special medley of people in whose close association on the campus was born a spirit that superseded race, culture, and creed. Together we were at the creation of three nations. Together we helped shape them. It was exciting to be involved in their education and as three hundred years of European dominance over Asia was ending, to witness the ponderous swing of history's pendulum ushering in the beginning of a new era of Asian independence.

Out of the thousands who between 1954 and 1966 were welcomed into the civil service, the professions, the commercial world, the armed services, and finally into the People's Action Party and government itself I mention a few known to me. They illustrate the breadth of our involvement.

Perhaps our most illustrious alumni was Goh Chok Tong, regrettably majoring in Economics in 1964 but despite this disadvantaged background becoming in time the Prime Minister of a flourishing state. Tony Tan was a political activist even as an undergraduate, a lecturer in Mathematics, later manager of the OCBC then elected to Parliament to become Minister of Education. S. Dhanabalan was another early Economics graduate who in 1961 was a member of the newly-formed Economic Development Board which under Dr Goh Keng Swee's drive was doing an amazing job in industrialising Singapore. Later he succeeded S. Rajaratnam as Foreign Minister. From my own department, Wong Lin Ken was Singapore's ambassador at the UN and later, Minister for Home Affairs. Chiang Hai Ding and Joe Conceicao I have mentioned earlier.

And there were others who joined Maurice Baker, Lau Teck Soon, Png Poh Seng, George Bogaars, Param Ajit Singh to serve in various ways the country in public service, while to give the list some sexual balance Daisy Chang Heng Swee, who graduated in 1964, was to become one of the nations top ambassadors and a university professor. The list, of medicos, teachers, lawyers, bankers and business men, soldiers and police officers, could be continued. Suffice to say that had it not been for our graduates, Singapore would not be here today.

Home

S ingapore, January 20, 1967. A Tanjong Pagar godown shelters us. Rain falls as we peer out at our ship, the *Centaur*, soon to sail. A new vessel, she has replaced the old *Gorgon* that brought me here some 14 years ago. I had seen her plans when interviewing her Blue Funnel executives in Liverpool some years earlier, collecting material on The Straits Steamship Company. She is making ready to return me to Fremantle. With the rain drifting over us, we scurry on board — five excited girls, their mother and me.

I lean on the rail and survey the familiar scene. Far up the harbour is Pulau Hantu (ghost island), a small nub of land around which I had raced in our open 16 foot skiff once a year for over a decade. Tacking up the harbour, I reflect, and the return to the yacht club (demolished by now, to make room for a container terminal) was always a challenge. Ships come and go, strong tides ebb and flow, winds drop or blow always in a crowded waterway. It all made for an enjoyable Sunday morning, with tiffin to follow.

Across the harbour is Pulau Brani, a small island where for several weeks early each morning years before I had been ferried over by a company launch to collect data for my history of what then was the world's greatest tin smelter, the Straits Trading Company. As I glance at it a 20,000 ton freighter moves past us, I see another at our western entrance near Blakang Mati (home of the useless guns of World War II) and I recall that over a hundred ship movements, in or out, occur each day. Singapore is on course to be the third or second busiest port in the world.

Soon enough the gang plank is hoisted and we cast off. My colleagues and friends fold their umbrellas and wave goodbye. They have agreed to take over the *Journal of Southeast Asian History*, which I had founded some years before, and my initial Conference of Southeast Asian Historians, to be held always in Asia, was very much alive in their hands. Wang Gungwu, Wong Lin Ken, Chiang Hai Ding, Png Poh Seng, Sharom Ahmat, R. Suntharalingam, young Edwin Lee, Eunice Thio and others were men and women of quality. All would be well.

We are under way, pushing steadily south through waters known so well to me. The rain has lifted and a rare rainbow is over Singapore. "That's a sign that we'll come back", I say to Jenni, my 13-year-old daughter. We did return, several times for her and her four sisters, more often for me, but in fact this is the end of my Singapore career. My immersion in the turbulent decade just past, and the history of this small island with its great people, surging now with self-confidence, is over. It had been a privilege to work here, to learn, to help, to absorb the Asian ethos and to watch the slow ponderous swing of history as the European era ended and that of Asia began. Now it was time to go.

There is a saying, "for your children you can do two things. You can give them roots and you can give them wings." The choice that at one stage or another all expatriates must choose, of country of calling, had been faced by me several years earlier. After years of excellent primary schooling, secondary school facilities for non-Singapore citizens then were negligible. My eldest daughter already was enrolled in her mother's old school in Western Australia, her sisters close behind. Hong Kong, New York and Melbourne all had offered me positions of academic and financial benefit, over-impressed at that remote distance by my eleven books and numerous journal articles, but as I glance at my girls my choice of home gives me no regrets.

A challenging future waits for me. I am to be headmaster of my old school, Hale. I have no experience of the responsibilities of this very exposed position. Four senior staff, all of whom had taught me, have reassured me of their loyalty and promised help in handling the 50 or so unsuspecting others and the 800 odd students on whom I have been imposed. I had in mind the words of St. Paul as he said to the Corinthians, "I have been given authority to lift you up" and I am to take this as my prime motivation (as it had been in the Singapore vanishing behind me).

The steward seats us for lunch. We are joined by an elderly Chinese gentleman and his wife. Courteously we exchange cards. He turns mine over to read the Chinese characters. "We have met before," he says "but where?" I can offer no answer. We all choose the Chinese meal. I manoeuvre my chopsticks with — though I say it myself — some dexterity. He is excited, "Yes, yes, you are left-handed! No Chinese uses his left hand with food, no Chinese is left-handed! That is where I met you, I remember, I too have lunched at the OCBC — you must be a friend of Mr Lee."

Dato Lee Kong Chian was our Chancellor. He was also the wealthiest *towkay* in all Southeast Asia, and one of the most generous. The Lee Foundation was well known for its beneficence. It had enabled me to launch the *Journal of Southeast Asian History* and it had helped bring many Asian academics to my international conference. Dato Lee had taken to inviting me on an occasional basis to lunch high up in the executive suite of his Overseas Chinese Banking Corporation building. He would talk of his early years, how he came in 1902 as a penniless migrant, his work with and marriage to the daughter of another famous man, Tan Kah Kee, how he cut off his queue before the 1911 revolution against the Manchus, his life-long interest in education — he had contributed millions to Nanyang University and the Chinese High School, and now was likewise supporting the University of Singapore, and as we ate, he would milk me of gossip about my Asian colleagues, and the university generally, while his — to my mind inscrutable — colleagues seated around this large circular table, would watch with well concealed horror my left-handed attempts at having a good meal.

"I think you all thought I was a Left-wing deviationary," I tell my companion. "No, no," he replies, "we had never seen a left-handed man before and yes we did wonder how an English speaking professor had won such support from Mr Lee. Not many sat at that table, I assure you." "We were united in helping Singaporeans," I replied, "our different backgrounds counted for nothing with the Dato." He is impressed. Clearly I have earned much face. But I am now to lose it. He glances at my daughters. Sympathetically he enquires, "No sons yet?"

When my wife had our first child, born in Kandang Kerbau hospital on March 20, 1954, the woman in the next bed was weeping uncontrollably. Giving birth to a girl, her husband had flung off in disgust and had flown to Hong Kong to find another wife who would give him a son. And in our early days the discarded body of a baby recovered from Rochore or Bukit Timah canal inevitably, so we were told, was a girl. I could not share this attitude. Daughters, I remember telling the *towkay*, are gifts from God. Fortunate are fathers with one, let alone with five. He is not impressed.

I had rebelled against this male chauvinism which lies deep within the Chinese psyche for over a decade. I remembered, as we played with our chopsticks, of the many girls who had been pioneer undergraduates, the first of their race in some cases, and what a delight it was to have them. In the early 1950s when our students included Malayans, there had been the three A's: Adibah Amin, Asiah bte Abu Samah, and Azizah bte Abbas. Ranu Battacharya was another, but her fiery nature made me wonder if her descendants came from Kerala. J. Kathirithamby who became a lecturer at Kuala Lumpur, she and others, many in their charming *sarong* and blouse, or *baju* (no head scarves then) were a credit to their nation. So too the Singapore girls. I recalled in particular Lucy Maniam, a tutor in our department, Cheng U Wen (who was a life-long friend), and others. Lucky the country that had them, I thought. To disparage their sex was to weaken the state.

An incident concerning the birth registration of my fourth daughter Margaret — or was it Fiona the fifth, who followed close behind? — came to mind. The clerk at the Registry Office began belting out my name "Professor K.G. Tregonning, University of Singapore" on his ancient typewriter as soon as I fronted up to the counter. I thought he must be a former student, and bent down to ask his name. "Oh no," he said "I remember you from last year. You had better go to the Family Planning Exhibition over in Victoria Hall." So I wandered over. Lee Kuan Yew's government was anxious to cut the birthrate, then over 4 per cent each year. A packed hall of slow moving townsfolk gawked at garish pictures of a half-starved man and a haggard wife trying to cope with four, five or more children. A healthy young man and his attractive wife held the hands of two sturdy boys. Other panels in basic colours showed in graphic detail how this could be achieved. Suitably admonished, I went home. (The exhibition, incidentally, along with other measures was a great success. Singapore's birth rate dropped markedly, leading the way in Asia.)

None of my children, alas, were baptised in Singapore, as I sailed every Sunday morning, and this was too important to cancel. We were to remedy this years later before they were married. None of them either were scarred by the turmoil that marked their youth. They may have seen the packs of angry rioters roaring as they burned vehicles in Bukit Timah Road beneath us, heard the swish of armoured cars on wet roads as the British army came over from Malaya, seen the barbed wire and the helmeted police at barricaded street junctions, even watched the thick palls of smoke rise into the sky from a city burning in the 1961 riots as they played in their garden. But it affected them not at all.

Rather the pattern of their lives had been shaped by the comforting regularity of their daily routine and enriched by the cosmopolitan and multi-racial environment that surrounded them. I would hope one day they might write their own memoirs. Their recollections could well differ from mine for children's thoughts are secret thoughts, known only to them. But of the life we shared surely, I thought, they would remember the racket of Chinese New Year when amid the din of crackers exploding, our *amahs* (Chinese servants who cared for children) would go off for three days, each given her *ang bao*, the traditional money gift in a red envelope. Perhaps also they would recall the Chinese mooncake festival, when candlelit lanterns glowed gently in their bedrooms. They had witnessed with me, deep inside the Sri Mariamman Temple, the climax of Thaipusam, when Hindu devotees, their backs, chests, sometimes their tongues pierced by thin needles or lances, would stagger in, half drugged with religious ecstasy, heavy *kavadis* on their sweat stained shoulders.

The Moslem Hari Raya Puasa, the end of the fasting month, was a much gentler affair, with the best sarongs worn and homemade cakes given to friends. Deepavali, the Festival of Lights, was another charming occasion, shared with our Indian *kebun*, or gardener. And, of course, preceded by carols in the Garrison Church, each child bringing a present, the festival celebrated by all, whatever their faith, Christmas.

In addition to these festivals I'm sure the daily happenings would stay in their memory. Our amahs taught them to count in Cantonese, occasionally took them to a *wayang*, the traditional Chinese opera on a street corner stage. There were birthday parties with the *gulli gulli* man (Indian conjuror and snake charmer), where presents were given to all who came, expeditions to Changi beach, where circling planes of the RAF waited for Sukarno to come, or the MacRitchie reservoir or, further afield when the Emergency had ended, to Malacca and Port Dickson; and above all perhaps, weekly fun at the Tanglin Club's swimming pool. There were visits to Barkaths, the Indian shop in Tanglin Road, where these little fair-headed children always attracted attention, inexpensive drawing pads purchased across the road near the tailor shop of my friend, Sardhar Tara Singh, whose son became a life-long friend, ice-cream at the Singapore Cold Storage in Orchard Road with its Nepalese trinket sellers outside, late afternoon toast on the lawn at the Royal Singapore Yacht Club near the harbour, where one watched the ever bustling anchorage and the occasional venture into town to wander in Change Alley, where the children would vanish unconcernedly in the maze of stalls.

School, of course, came to play a prominent part in their lives. The Tanglin School was happy and well run. Expatriate staff, mainly English, and its management Board set high standards — at least a year ahead, so we discovered of those in Western Australia — so that English children on return home could enjoy their parents' six-month leave, as it was then and still qualify for secondary school. It finished at midday, when their mother would collect them (by now a Holden had replaced our Morris Minor) and call for me.

By the 1960s we had become entitled to a compact, newly built two-storey home on Leyden Hill, part of a university enclave of Senior Staff: Chinese, Indian, European. Lim Tay Bo, our Vice-chancellor, was a near neighbour and good friend. Three bed-rooms upstairs, with windows to the floor and balcony, a lounge-dining area and kitchen below with servants quarters attached. The access road was a dead end, so the children and their friends could ride their bikes along it without fear. Our front lawn with its hibiscus and canna flowers and the occasional snake, ended where the little hill dropped steeply down to the Dunearn Road student quarters. I often had walked home in the late afternoon from the university, to cross Bukit Timah road and canal (often flooded in those early days) and looking up, could see five children waving and coming down to meet me. The vista from our hilltop home of palm trees and greenery far away added to the charms of our reunion; while sometimes we hurried inside as the wind and rain of the Sumatra came sweeping across.

A cold shower, a *stengah* or two of whiskey and water as we sat outside in the comparative cool of the early evening, Brahms or Greig drifting upstairs to where the children were falling asleep. For me, home and work had been blended in that decade into creative and tranquil happiness. As *Centaur* sailed south, and Singapore fell behind, merdeka memories indeed.

Index